THE GENEVA CONSENSUS

The Geneva Consensus highlights the vital role that open trade plays in generating global economic growth, a key condition for reducing poverty and creating jobs around the world. But trade can only act as a motor for growth if the correct mix of domestic and international economic and social policies is also in place. This approach – described as the 'Geneva Consensus' – requires deeper co-operation and policy coherence between the various international organizations active in setting or seeking to mould international economic, social and political policies.

    The Geneva Consensus describes what has been done and what remains to be done to put this consensus into effect, and calls for more effective global governance to tackle the challenges of globalization. It also examines how trade relates to and influences key social, economic and political issues of our time, such as health, climate change, human rights or currency volatility.

PASCAL LAMY was Director-General of the World Trade Organization from 2005 until 2013. Between 1999 and 2004, he was the European Commissioner for Trade.

THE GENEVA CONSENSUS

Making Trade Work for All

PASCAL LAMY

CAMBRIDGE
UNIVERSITY PRESS

CAMBRIDGE
UNIVERSITY PRESS

University Printing House, Cambridge CB2 8BS, United Kingdom

Published in the United States of America by Cambridge University Press, New York

Cambridge University Press is part of the University of Cambridge.

It furthers the University's mission by disseminating knowledge in the pursuit of education, learning and research at the highest international levels of excellence.

www.cambridge.org
Information on this title: www.cambridge.org/9781107053069

© Pascal Lamy 2013

First published 2013

Printed in the United Kingdom by Clays, St Ives plc

A catalogue record for this publication is available from the British Library

Library of Congress Cataloguing-in-Publication Data
Lamy, P. (Pascal)
The Geneva consensus : making trade work for all / Pascal Lamy.
    pages cm
ISBN 978-1-107-05306-9 (Hardback) – ISBN 978-1-107-66415-9 (pbk.)
1. Lamy, P. (Pascal) 2. World Trade Organization. 3. International trade.
4. Developing countries–Commercial treaties. I. Title.
HF1385.L35 2014
382'.92–dc23   2013039597

ISBN 978-1-107-05306-9 Hardback
ISBN 978-1-107-66415-9 Paperback

CONTENTS

v

In 1999, as I was preparing to appear before the European Parliament to make my case for becoming the European Union Trade Commissioner, I decided to use the term 'harnessing globalization'. It was intended to capture the ultimate objective of international trade and economic policies at the turn of the century. It became central to my tenure as EU Trade Commissioner. It continued to be my guiding principle during my eight years as Director-General of the World Trade Organization (WTO). Globalization continues to unleash incredible transformational power in our societies, thanks in particular to scientific and technological advances. But this power needs to be harnessed, to be channelled, to be tamed, if we want globalization to be for the benefit of all.

Trade has been an extremely efficient conveyor belt of globalization. It has been a powerful instrument for promoting growth and development, for reducing poverty and for improving standards of living. And the WTO has been an essential instrument in harnessing global trade. It has been the key forum where trade opening has been negotiated and where the rules governing global trade and trade disputes among countries have been set. It is a successful example of global governance.

This book is a collection of memories from my eight years at the helm of the WTO. I have largely drawn from articles and speeches I delivered in my role as chief advocate for the values and objectives of the multilateral trading system. The range of topics covered is selective in that it reflects my own choice of issues I wish to explore. I have essentially chosen those that I believe are the most important for understanding the complex task of making trade work for growth and development.

I fundamentally believe that trade opening is essential for achieving growth and development, but the benefits resulting from open trade depend on the quality of policies in other areas. This is what I have dubbed the 'Geneva Consensus', a term I first used when I campaigned to become WTO Director-General in 2005. It centres on recognizing the incredible powers of trade openness and fair trade rules for all. But it also recognizes that trade opening, with all the benefits and also the occasional hardships that it brings, has to be embedded in a wider framework of domestic and international policies. I call this the 'Geneva' Consensus, as this city is home to both the WTO and the United Nations and embodies the very idea of a society of nations working together towards a shared goal.

The WTO cannot be an ivory tower. The high priests of international trade cannot remain ensconced in the comfort of their beautiful Lake Geneva headquarters. The WTO must integrate its work into the agenda of governments, civil society and other international organizations that are working for growth and development so that this work brings about positive results, and not just theoretical assertions. And the members of the WTO – 159 governments across the globe – must do their part by ensuring that trade opening is at the core of their domestic and international policies.

Trade opening today is much more than just lowering tariffs and establishing tariff quotas. It is much more than just goods and services. In fact, today it is often difficult to distinguish between a good and a service. It is also about the interactions between trade and the environment, health, food security, jobs, even human rights. It is about how trade and currencies interact. It is also about how open trade is embedded into a framework of fairer global competition. Finally, trade opening is not just about creating opportunities. It is also about ensuring that opportunities translate into results by helping developing countries improve their capacity to trade.

An account of my eight years at the WTO would not be complete without mentioning the Doha Development Round. As I write this book, there is a very strong likelihood that this collective endeavour to update the rules of global trade could be given a decisive push with the adoption of a deal on trade facilitation – reducing 'red tape' for the exchange of goods and services across borders – at the WTO's Ninth Ministerial Conference in Indonesia in December 2013. The chapter on the adventures and misadventures of the Doha Round comes at the end of this book. This is not intended to indicate in any way a lack of importance. It is just that the twelve preceding chapters provide the background for understanding the difficulties surrounding multilateral trade negotiations today and why it has proved to be so difficult to conclude the Doha Round.

This book would not have been possible without the support and dedication of my Chief of Staff during these eight years, Arancha González. Her observations and advice have been of immense value to me. My thanks also go to Doaa Abdel-Motaal, Emmanuelle Ganne, Xiaodong Wang and Matthew Wilson in my office at the WTO, and to Anthony Martin, Chief Editor at the WTO.

Pascal Lamy
Geneva, August 2013

1

Harnessing globalization amid the crisis facing multilateralism

One of my first trips on becoming WTO Director-General in 2005 was to Chile. I went at the invitation of my old friend and then Chilean President Ricardo Lagos, a fellow Social Democrat and someone who had thought hard about globalization and its advantages and drawbacks. Chile was then and is now one of the most open economies in Latin America. It has been one of the most successful in achieving economic growth, although it continues to face significant economic and social challenges, such as growing inequality. One of President Lagos's major concerns was how to 'humanize' the phenomenon of globalization so that its benefits would be felt as widely as possible among all strata of society and become a force for social and economic development. It was to be one of my prime concerns throughout my time at the WTO.

Globalization has enabled individuals, corporations and nation states to influence activities around the world – making the exchange of goods and services faster, deeper and cheaper than ever before. Globalization can be defined as a historic expansion of market capitalism, comparable in many respects to the Industrial Revolution of the nineteenth century. It is a fundamental transformation of society brought about largely by the ongoing technological revolution. Globalization has led to the disappearance of many barriers: it has the potential to expand freedom, democracy, innovation and

1

social and cultural exchanges, while offering huge opportunities for greater dialogue and understanding.

But the global nature of an increasing number of worrisome phenomena – the scarcity of energy resources, the deterioration of the environment and the spread of pandemics (AIDS, bird flu), the growing interdependence of economies and financial markets and the ensuing knock-on effect of financial crises, and greater movement across borders provoked by insecurity, poverty or political instability – are also a product of globalization.

Nobody would dispute that there is a widening gap between global challenges and the traditional working methods of our international institutions. What can we do to bridge this gap? Some advocate de-globalization: let's turn our backs on globalization, let's lessen our interdependence and the world will get better! I do not think this can work. It is neither possible, nor desirable. It is not possible because the main engine of globalization is technological progress, and technology moves forwards, not backwards. And it is not desirable either. Who would want to give up the benefits that come with globalization? Should we stop travelling by plane to avoid the spread of pandemics? Are we ready to renounce our cherished mobile phone and Internet connection? Should we put a halt to global production chains (see Chapter 2), which have helped so many developing countries to benefit from open trade? The reality we live in has its downsides, but it has many advantages. It is illusory to think we can turn our backs on globalization.

So what option do we have but to increase our capacity to manage global challenges by improving global governance? We must harness globalization so that it becomes a force that promotes human development. And harnessing globalization has been my 'work in progress' for a long time.

The fall of the Berlin Wall in 1989 was a turning point in globalization. The end of the Cold War led to an unprecedented era of economic openness. We saw a reduction in poverty like never before. Freedom expanded and with it ideas, culture and technology. And yet over twenty years later the world is in a state of serious distress. We are struggling to emerge from the worst-ever economic crisis and the first such crisis to have a global reach; a crisis that has seen the decimation of employment. We are seeing our planet deteriorate due to global warming, with severe droughts and violent floods and entire islands disappearing under water. We face the awful threat of nuclear proliferation.

The fact is that the end of the Cold War caught everyone by surprise. It was the end of a bipolar world. A new world order was born, but there was not enough thinking and discussion about global governance. Post 1989, there was no equivalent to the Bretton Woods Conference of 1944, which laid the foundations for a new international financial order to follow World War Two, or the San Francisco Conference, which resulted in the United Nations Charter. As a result, global governance structures did not adjust. And here lies the root of many of today's problems. Global challenges need global solutions and these can only come with the right global governance, which today, twenty years later, remains too weak.

New forms of global governance

The new issues being raised by global crises and by certain political developments oblige us to contemplate new forms of governance. To address global questions, problems, threats, fears, at the appropriate level, we need more, and better, governance at the global level responsive to emerging global challenges. Global governance should be understood as the system that helps a global society achieve its common purposes in a sustainable manner – that is, with equity and justice. Interdependence requires that our laws, our social norms and values, and other mechanisms for framing human behaviour – family, education, culture, religion, to name only a few of them – be examined, understood and operated together as coherently as possible so as to ensure our collective, effective sustainable development.

The term 'governance' was first used in twelfth-century France, where it was a technical term designating the administration of baillages, or bailiwicks. As with the word 'government', it comes from the Latin word for 'rudder', conveying the idea of steering. From France, it crossed the Channel and in England came to designate the method of organizing feudal power. Underlying feudal power were adjacent 'suzerainties', among which there had to be coherence. There was no central power as such, but a body, *primus inter pares*, whose purpose was to settle disputes peacefully and see that any conflicting interests were reconciled by consultation with those involved. Governance, which largely disappeared as a concept in the sixteenth century with the emergence of the nation state, thus focused on unity – not uniqueness – of interests. If we liken international society to a medieval society in its lack of any organized central power, then it needs governance. In other words, it needs a concept that affords a basis for the organization of power, or the elements of consultation and dialogue necessary to secure greater harmony. The discrepancy between today's interdependence, the challenges resulting from it and the capacity of governments to agree politically on how to deal with it is striking. The international system is founded on the principle and politics of national sovereignty: the nation state is the principal actor on the international stage. This is known as the 'Westphalian' order – named after the treaties of 1648 that put an end to Europe's Thirty Years War – and it remains very much alive in the international architecture of today. In the absence of a truly global government, global governance results from the action of sovereign states. It is inter-national, between nations. In other words, global governance is the globalization of local governance. But it is not enough to establish groupings or specialized international organizations to ensure a coherent and efficient approach to the global problems of our time. In fact, the Westphalian order is a challenge in itself. The recent crisis has demonstrated it brutally. Local politics have taken the upper hand over addressing global issues. Governments are too busy dealing with domestic issues to dedicate sufficient attention and energy to multilateral negotiations, be they trade negotiations or climate negotiations.

During my professional life, I have had the opportunity to work at three different levels of governance, which I compare to the three states of mass: the national level, which in my view represents the solid state; the European level, which is liquid; and the international level, which is more like the gaseous mass. The challenge for global governance today is to try to move from its current gaseous state to a more solid one.

There are four main challenges facing the creation of an effective system of global governance today.

The first one is leadership, i.e. the capacity to embody a vision and inspire action, in order to create momentum. Who is the leader? Should it be a superpower? Should it be a group of national leaders? Selected by whom? Or should it be an international organization?

The second challenge is efficiency, by which I mean the capacity to mobilize resources, to solve problems in the international sphere and to bring about concrete and visible results for the benefit of the people. The main challenge here is that the Westphalian order gives an advantage to the 'naysayers', who can block decisions and prevent any results being achieved. The ensuing viscosity of international decision-making, and you have to look no further than the UN Security Council, puts into question the efficiency of the international system as its stands today.

The third challenge is coherence. The international system is based on specialization, with each international organization focusing on a limited number of issues. The WTO deals with trade, the International Labour Organization (ILO) with labour issues, the World Meteorological Organization (WMO) with meteorology and so on. There is a need to increase coherence in the actions taken within each of these international organizations.

6

The last challenge is that of legitimacy – for legitimacy is intrinsically linked to proximity, to a sense of 'togetherness'. By togetherness, I mean the shared feeling of belonging to a community. This feeling, which is generally strong at the local level, tends to weaken significantly as distance to power systems grows. It finds its roots in common myths, a common history and a collective cultural heritage. It is no surprise that taxation and redistribution policies remain mostly local!

There is one place where attempts to deal with these challenges have been made and where new forms of governance have been tested for the last sixty years: in Europe. The European construction is the most ambitious experiment in supra-national governance ever attempted. It is the story of a desired, delineated and organized interdependence between member states. How has this endeavour coped with the challenges I have just outlined? These are not easy times for the European integration process, with doubts emerging about its future course. I nevertheless believe that it teaches us valuable lessons for global governance.

Triangle of coherence

Here are a few pragmatic ideas for a possible way forward to bridge the global governance deficit. First, the European experience offers valuable lessons both in terms of institutions and tools. In terms of institutions, the European integration process shows that supra-national governance can work. Of course, this does not go without difficulties, and it is highly unlikely that what was done at the European level can be replicated as such at the international level. The European paradigm was developed under very specific conditions of temperature and pressure. It was shaped by the geographical and historical heritage of a European continent devastated by two world wars. Hence there was a collective aspiration for peace, stability and prosperity. It is my firm conviction, however, that when it comes to institutions at the global level, there is a way to articulate the three elements of governance – leadership, efficiency and legitimacy – through what I call the 'triangle of coherence'.

On one side of the triangle lies the G20 group of leading developed and developing countries, which has essentially replaced the former G8 that was made up of the seven leading Western industrialized states plus Russia. For decades the G7 and then the G8 had sought to provide some form of global leadership. The G20, which includes such developing countries as China, India, Brazil, Turkey, Indonesia, Mexico and Saudi Arabia, better reflects the current distribution of global economic power. The G20 can provide political leadership, policy direction and coherence. The second side of the triangle is the United Nations, which can offer global legitimacy through accountability. On the third side of the triangle lie the international organizations, which provide expertise and specialized knowledge.

This 'triangle' of global governance is emerging. Bridges linking the G20 to international organizations and to the UN system have started to be built. As WTO Director-General, I participated in G20 meetings, alongside the heads of a number of other international organizations. Specific sessions dedicated to trade have been regularly organized during G20 summits. The political backing of the G20 allowed me, at the dawn of the 2008 financial crisis, to launch a strengthened monitoring of trade policy developments within the WTO, which has proved a useful and powerful tool to contain protectionism.

In terms of tools, I believe that the European experience of rule-making, transparency and peer review offers interesting avenues for the global level. Peer review appears to me an efficient 'Westphalian' tool of governance. It leverages the pride and self-esteem of sovereign nations. Within the European Union it is used frequently, with the European Commission monitoring the actions of individual states in a number of policy areas, including the application of the rules of the single market, state aid to industries and environmental questions, to name just three. Globally there are also examples. The United Nations Human Rights Council, despite the criticism often levelled against it for being too 'politicized', ensures that the human rights record of every member state is periodically scrutinized. In other words, every country gets its day in the dock. The system of peer review needs to be used more widely, particularly in the economic sphere, where the UN's Economic and Social Council (ECOSOC) could play a greater role. Finally, one needs to pay more attention to values. Institutions alone cannot do the trick. Our experience with global governance to date demonstrates that. A successful system of governance requires not only institutions and tools, but also a common objective and shared values.

Common values

What is lacking today is a platform of common values at the international level, in the name of which actions are taken.

The question of social inequalities, for example, is not embodied in the UN vision as designed in the 1950s. Our world needs a platform of common values, which would be shared not only by the 'West', but also by the 'Rest'. Globalization brings into contact peoples and societies that have made historical choices that are sometimes similar, sometimes very different from one place to another. A debate about collective values, regional or universal, has become a necessity. This debate on shared values might allow us to define the common goods or benefits that we would like to promote and defend collectively on a global scale. Without a basic agreement of this kind, it is difficult to talk about global 'public goods'. Public goods – things that are perceived as beneficial in the sense that trade can be seen as a 'good' because it brings growth – are necessarily underpinned by common values.

If we are to address efficiently today's global challenges, which in many cases are related to the defence, promotion or protection of global public goods, we need to share a collective sense of values. In fact we need a new declaration of global rights and responsibilities – a global charter of values that goes beyond the Universal Declaration of Human Rights.

German Chancellor Angela Merkel, together with other leaders, suggested in 2009 that the G20 agree to the drawing up of a global charter for sustainable economic activity. The ILO, the International Monetary Fund (IMF), the Organisation for Economic Co-operation and Development (OECD), the World Bank and the WTO would have had the task of supporting the elaboration of the text. The G20 failed to agree on the plan in 2009, but perhaps in time some global understanding will emerge on what should unite all countries when it comes to economic policy making.

We must also reach out to civil society, unions, political parties and parliamentarians to discuss and debate with them the global issues we are facing. We need global governance, but effective global governance necessitates global citizens. It needs citizens imbued with a sense of belonging to a global community. How many people today, when asked which country they come from, would answer, like the ancient Greek philosopher Diogenes of Sinope, 'I am a citizen of the world'? In the absence of global elections, the global governance debate needs to be brought closer to citizens to instil the feeling of togetherness that is now missing. Bringing the global governance debate closer to citizens could make governments more accountable in terms of policy coherence.

But the last couple of years have seen the emergence of a worrying attitude towards multilateralism. In stark contrast to the calls for greater and improved international regulatory coherence that dominated the headlines at the start of the global financial crisis in 2008, international co-operation has slumped to an ever more precarious state. In high-income countries, a weak recovery and stubbornly high unemployment have made voters fearful that any gains made by faster-growing emerging economies are coming at their expense. This has made their political representatives even more reluctant to make what they see as 'concessions' to the likes of China, Brazil or India in international negotiations. Emerging economies have responded in kind, wary of losing hard-earned developmental gains. We have also seen turbulence in many emerging economies as their middle classes

11

demand more efficient and accountable government. The result has been that multilateral rule-making on issues ranging from trade governance to climate change, already struggling prior to the crisis, has come to a near halt.

The once widespread conviction that well-managed globalization could offer 'win–wins' for developed and developing countries now seems distant. Hopes of cooperative action to tackle environmental degradation appear to have dwindled. In the words of *Financial Times* columnist Gideon Rachman, the 'age of optimism' that reigned between the collapse of the Soviet Union and the fall of Lehman Brothers has given way to a 'zero-sum world'. Cynical observers of international relations would say that over the past decade, international efforts to forge legally binding agreements – such as on climate change – have continued to set the threshold of expectations so low that even an agreement to continue to talk is considered a successful outcome. In my view, such cynicism ignores the fundamental lessons about international co-operation that we have learned over the past century. Governance at the global level can only be built step by step. Most of all, it disregards the fact that for most countries more multilateralism and more international co-operation remain the only sustainable way forward.

Either multilateralism advances in the spirit of shared values and enhanced co-operation, or we will face a retreat from multilateralism, at our peril. Without global co-operation on finance, security, trade, the environment and poverty reduction, the risks of division, strife and war will remain dangerously real. Waiting for better times will simply not suffice. A consensus for inaction would simply mean a consensus for more pain for all. We must, together, be bolder to cope with growing risks.

Trade governance

One of the tools at hand to harness globalization is the multilateral trading system. But multilateralism is also at a crossroads when it comes to trade, with the WTO's Doha Round of trade negotiations still far from concluded. The Round is intended to rebalance the world trading system in favour of developing countries, through greater market opening and new trade rules adapted to the changing trading realities of the twenty-first century. But for a number of reasons, some of them economic, some of them geopolitical, it has not been possible to reach a deal in the talks, which were launched in the Qatari capital in November 2001. I will discuss in detail the difficulties behind this deadlock, and how they may be surmounted, in Chapter 13.

Partially in response to the lack of progress in the Doha negotiations, the last few years have seen the mushrooming of preferential trade agreements (PTAs), both bilateral and regional. PTAs have their advantages, but they cannot replace multilateral agreements when it comes to resolving global trade problems and providing global trade governance. For many small and poor developing countries, entering into a bilateral agreement with a powerful big country means less leverage and a weaker negotiating position than they would have within multilateral talks. This might not be the case for India, China, Brazil, the United States and the European Union, but it is for the likes of Mauritius, Sri Lanka, Cambodia or Ghana.

The WTO is a small governance system, which is underpinned by a common value, or belief, that market opening, framed by global rules, is good. Market opening allows for a division of labour between countries and for resources to be used more appropriately and more effectively for production. This view has been forged by observing the negative effects of protectionism on our economies at different times in recent history, and in particular between the two world wars of the last century, and comparing them with the positive effects of the opening up of trade in the last fifty years. But institutionally the WTO is weak. Decisions are taken by consensus, providing a de facto veto to each member, or at least to the most powerful ones. Unlike in the European Union, for instance, in the WTO there is no body entitled to initiate legislative change. The WTO Secretariat or the WTO councils and committees cannot enact regulations or other norms. This authority is left to states alone. It is the epitome of the Westphalian system.

Yet the WTO has put in place a few principles that recognize that the WTO is an international public good. First, its preamble states that while trade expansion should take place, it should do so 'allowing for the optimal use of the world's resources in accordance with the objective of sustainable development'. By definition, sustainable development calls for the consideration of fundamental values other than those of market opening, including, for instance, the protection of the environment, human rights and other social values. It also prohibits any unilateral action by any WTO member. No perceived violation of WTO accords permits resort to a unilateral retaliatory measure by a member.

If members disagree as to whether a WTO violation has occurred, they can take the matter to the dispute settlement process and obtain a ruling.

Furthermore, the WTO's top court, the Appellate Body, has ruled that WTO provisions cannot be read in 'clinical isolation' from international law. This sets the WTO firmly within a more global system that includes several sets of rights and obligations. There is no priority given to WTO norms over others covering health and the environment, for example. Hence the need to ensure global coherence in the interpretation and application of all values, rights and obligations. But the obligation to seek coherence with other international organizations extends beyond the judicial. If trade opening results in a different distribution of benefits between nations, then that is something that the WTO can seek to resolve. But if it is a question of the distribution of benefits within nations, then that is a matter beyond its control. It is an issue that requires policy coherence, both at the national and the international level.

Geneva Consensus

Open global markets are essential sources of demand and know-how for achieving rapid catch-up growth. But economists have always known that the benefits of trade are not distributed evenly across nations or within nations. History teaches us that trade reform meets social resistance if the distribution of gains from trade is too uneven. Trade opening is neither natural nor automatically beneficial, in and of itself. While the opening up of markets, stimulated by the WTO as the home of multilateral trade negotiations, has the potential to produce benefits for many, it also has its costs, whose distribution is largely beyond the control of the WTO.

Trade opening is a necessary condition for economic growth, but it is not a sufficient one. For trade opening to work, it needs to be accompanied by assistance to the poorest countries to build up their productive and logistical capacities so they can benefit from new markets. They also need assistance in increasing their capacity to negotiate and to implement commitments undertaken in the international trading system. Finally, help is needed in dealing with the imbalances created between winners and losers from trade opening – imbalances that are more dangerous in the more fragile economies, societies or countries. Building the capacity of developing countries to take advantage of open markets and helping them to adjust is now part of the WTO agenda – it is what I have dubbed the 'Geneva Consensus'.

The Geneva Consensus seeks to supply the international policy coherence on matters relating to trade that we have identified as being a vital ingredient of good governance. It is through the Geneva Consensus that we have tried to ensure that the policies of international organizations active in issues relating to trade and development – which can range from financing and capacity building to health and intellectual property (IP) rights – are co-ordinated and have a common aim so that we are, in essence, 'singing from the same hymn sheet'.

It was Ricardo Lagos who got me thinking about the need for this new approach. I recall him saying on that visit to Santiago in 2005 that the so-called 'Washington Consensus' on economic reform, which was still very much in vogue in Latin America at the time, was only half of the story. 'The Washington Consensus was only about structural reforms. But we should not forget the other part, which is making sure that people are able to benefit from these reforms', he told me. Unlike the Washington Consensus, a term coined in the late 1980s for the essentially open-market economic advice, including fiscal discipline and trade liberalization, being given by Washington-based institutions to developing countries, the Geneva Consensus lays emphasis on the need to build up the supply side and create capacity to trade and to trade well, but also the capacity to better address the costs of, and better distribute the benefits of, trade opening. It is 'Geneva' for the obvious reason that the WTO and many of the organizations in the United Nations family have established their headquarters in Geneva. Some of the challenges that the Geneva Consensus sets can be met within the WTO. But the WTO's core role is trade opening and it lacks the institutional capacity to formulate and lead development strategies. Bringing the benefits of trade opening to all requires the involvement of other actors on the international economic policy scene, such as the UN family, the Bretton Woods institutions and regional development banks.

Fortunately, much has been done in recent years to promote policy coherence in assisting developing countries to trade. Many of these initiatives will be dealt with in subsequent chapters. But let me just give an example. One extremely important initiative that improves the ability of developing countries to trade is called, logically enough, Aid for Trade. Launched by trade ministers in 2005, it has so far raised billions of dollars for projects to help developing countries, particularly least-developed countries (LDCs), integrate more into the global trading system. Another initiative aimed at assisting developing countries to trade is the Standards and Trade Development Facility (STDF), a five-agency programme that helps developing countries meet international standards on food safety and animal and plant health. I will have more to say on Aid for Trade and the STDF in Chapter 3.

To conclude, multilateralism is struggling, as is the Doha Round, and global governance is still woefully lacking. But trade-related international organizations have striven through the Geneva Consensus to develop one side of the governance triangle – that of policy coherence – and to make a difference to people's lives, equipping poorer developing countries to benefit from the rapidly changing pattern of global trade.

2

The changing face of trade

In December 2012, I flew to Samoa to visit the small Pacific island state that had become the WTO's 155th member earlier in the year. Of course, I had expected the coconut groves, bright colours and white sandy beaches that are everybody's idea of what a South Sea island paradise should have. But I was less prepared for what I witnessed at the Yazaki EDS plant in Apia, the capital of Samoa. Hundreds of Samoans work at the Yazaki factory, which is the country's largest industrial employer. Led through the plant by its Japanese manager, I saw thousands of coloured wires being hand-strung into bundles called harnesses, which make up a crucial part of the electronic nervous system of cars and trucks. The wire harnesses are then sent along the Asia-Pacific trade routes to Japan to be inserted into Toyota vehicles that are shipped to all corners of the world. Deep in the southern seas, thousands of kilometres from any major market, was a well-oiled and organized cog in a global production chain. It is an example of the emerging new face of world trade.

Global trade has changed profoundly in the past decade or so. The changes are being driven partly by market opening, but mainly by transport, communications and information technologies. It now costs less to ship a container from Marseille to Shanghai – halfway around the world – than to move it from Marseille to Avignon – 100 kilometres away in southern France. One result of these changes is the continuing globalization of trade, with the volume and value of international commerce continuing to expand, extending trade's economic influence to all corners of the world. Another consequence is the rapid shift in economic power to the East and South, as developing countries harness globalization to 'catch up' with the industrialized West. Finally, we are witnessing the spread of globally integrated production chains, or value chains – in effect, global factories – as companies place various stages of the production process – such as wire harnesses for vehicles – in the most cost-efficient places. This latter development has immense consequences for the way we view and measure trade, which in turn has important implications for international trade policy.

Despite the recent crisis, world exports were 66 per cent higher in 2010 than in 2000 – and 230 per cent higher than in 1990. Not all sectors are expanding at the same pace: raw material exports have grown more than food exports and manufactured goods. But overall the trend is towards accelerating growth. With few exceptions, trade between regions is growing faster than trade within regions. Never before has the world economy been as inter-linked by trade as it is today.

Twenty years ago, 60 per cent of world trade was between developed countries (North–North), 30 per cent was between developed and developing countries (North–South) and 10 per cent was South–South. By 2020, we are expecting it to be split equally three ways, so the relative weight of North–North trade will have been halved in just thirty years or so. In 1990, less than a third of developing-country trade was with other developing countries; today over half of their trade is South–South. Developing countries are now the largest market for other developing countries. Developing countries' share of total exports jumped from 33 per cent to 43 per cent over the first decade of this century, with China's exports growing at a staggering 20 per cent a year. Developing countries' share of total world trade – including both imports and exports – has grown from a third to over half in just fifteen years – and China has overtaken Japan as the world's second biggest national economy, and Germany as the world's top exporter.

While this growth in South–South trade is encouraging, it is skewed. Asian countries make up more than 80 per cent of South–South trade with the shares of Africa and Latin America being just 6 per cent and 10 per cent respectively in 2010. Not all developing countries, therefore, are sharing in this trade growth, and for too many, the concerns of Argentine Economist Raúl Prebisch – expressed some sixty years ago – about dependency and an uneven playing field for trade remain true. But for export power-houses like China, India, Brazil and others – growing at historically unprecedented rates – Prebisch's fears that developing countries would always lose out in trade with the rich industrialized countries are being turned on their head.

A similar picture of the shifting composition of global economic power emerges with respect to foreign direct investment (FDI). While global FDI inflows have – on average – increased by 6 per cent over the last decade, developing countries' share has risen from around 25 per cent to almost 45 per cent. Further evidence comes from the changing map of global greenhouse gas emissions. Emissions of the developing world are rising fast and China's emissions are said to be at least equal to those of the United States. The International Energy Agency tells us that even if OECD countries were to bring their emissions down to zero, the world would still be likely to miss its temperature containment target of an extra two degrees Celsius during the course of this century.

The emergence of developing countries as key players and as real contributors to global dialogue on trade and economics is a fundamental feature of the new geopolitical reality. These emerging powers – Brazil, Chile, China, India, Indonesia, Malaysia, Mexico, South Africa, Thailand, Turkey and others – are no longer policy takers. These countries now increasingly influence the pattern and scope of international trade, creating new supply and demand centres of gravity and flexing their influence in international organizations. In addition to the reconfiguration of the actors in the multilateral trading system and the changing patterns of trade, we are also seeing new trends in the way that goods and services are produced and traded. There is a new narrative developing on trade. Governments and business have to take notice of this and align their policies and priorities around it.

Ricardo's port

In the nineteenth century, when English economist David Ricardo developed what was to become the foundation of the theory of international trade, countries exported what they produced. Ricardo used the famous example of the exchange of an English manufactured good – cloth – for Port wine. The production of cloth made of wool from English sheep enabled the English to drink good wine, while the

Portuguese had clothes to wear thanks to their winemaking skills. For many decades, until well after the first effects of the Industrial Revolution had been felt, the cloth and wine example continued to be relevant, since all of the inputs and services required for the manufacture of goods came from the same country. The Industrial Revolution began in Great Britain, a country that had coal and iron mines as well as a significant urban population ready to work in the factories. If you bought a steam engine in England, you could be sure that all of the parts, from the steel of the wheels to the boiler pressure gauges, came from Great Britain.

A lot has changed since then. Port wine is still of Portuguese origin, and thanks to the WTO's designation of origin regulations, an English importer has better guarantees in that respect than his nineteenth-century ancestors. But the country of origin concept for manufactured goods became more and more obsolete as companies began to resort first to local subcontractors, and then to international subcontractors for jobs or tasks that they did not consider – or no longer considered – to belong to their 'core business', as they call it in business circles. Today, the expansion of global value or production chains means that most products are assembled with inputs from many countries. We may still think in terms of Ricardo's world of trade between nations, but in reality most trade now takes place within globe-spanning multi-national companies and their suppliers.

The results of this 'trade in tasks' are all around us. Take an iPhone. The legend inscribed on the back of an iPhone declares 'Designed by Apple in California. Assembled in China.' This does not do justice to parts made in China,

South Korea, Japan, Germany, and the United States, by companies headquartered in Tokyo, Seoul, Bavaria, San Diego, Stuttgart, Texas and Geneva. The parts are assembled in Shenzhen, China, by a company from Chinese Taipei. It is not competition between China and the United States that is relevant so much as competition between Nokia's and Samsung's value chains. Instead of 'Assembled in China' on the back of an iPhone, the label should read 'Made in the World', reflecting the Japanese microchips, US design, South Korean flat-screens, as well as the assembling in China, that have contributed to the final product. Much the same goes for the iPads being put together in Chengdu, as I witnessed when I travelled to the Foxconn factory in 2011.

With value chains, it is no longer necessary to be competitive in producing a particular product or service; it is enough to be competitive in delivering a particular task. This has the added advantage of reducing dramatically the cost to smaller economies of joining the global trading system. Value chains can help developing landlocked countries, such as Botswana, Lao PDR or Mongolia, for example, to overcome the geographical disadvantages that could in the past limit their participation in world trade. The growing weight of services in the business portfolios of developing countries and the increase in the reach of technology and transportation are fast narrowing the distances between and to markets and creating new opportunities for these countries to grow through trade.

In 2013 the WTO, at the urging of developing countries, devoted its annual review of its initiative on Aid for Trade, which is assistance specifically geared to helping poor countries trade more and better (see Chapter 3), to the question of connecting to value chains. The fact that value chains were chosen by developing countries as the theme for the review shows the extent to which these countries have realized just how far value chains are changing the face of trade.

Today, almost 60 per cent of trade in goods is in intermediates, which are goods used as inputs in a further production process. An important consequence of the integration of production networks is that imports matter as much as exports when it comes to contributing to job creation and to economic growth. In 1990, the import content of exports was 20 per cent; in 2010, it was 40 per cent, and it is expected to be around 60 per cent in 2030. This is why enacting 'protectionist' measures in the modern world to protect jobs, such as raising import barriers, can have an inverse reaction in economies that are increasingly reliant on imports to complete their exports. This narrative is already transforming the policy debate on trade and should lead to more nuanced and evidence-based decisions that reflect more truly the impact that trade can have on growth, employment and innovation. In effect, we are seeing the end of the centuries-old doctrine of 'mercantilism', which proclaimed that a country's economic strength depended on it being able to export more than it imported.

Today, the production of goods and services is 'multi-located'; a new 'invention of the world' in the words of Jacques Lévy, Professor of Geography at the École Polytechnique Fédérale de Lausanne (EPFL). As a result, the notion of 'relocation', which has people trembling in Western countries, loses much of its meaning. If I relocate a segment of the production chain for reasons of economies of scale, and others relocate to my area for the same reasons, the impact on my total value added, i.e. roughly speaking, my ability to create or maintain jobs, may be neutral, negative or positive. Nowadays, it is this balance that counts.

All this confirms that the way we measure trade needs to change. Our traditional methodology assigns the total commercial value of an import to a single country of origin. This was an accurate formula when trade just involved final goods produced from domestic inputs. It might even have worked when imported raw materials were processed in a single country. But when applied to 'Made in the World' products, such as the iPhone mentioned earlier, the methodology can exaggerate bilateral trade balances and understate where value addition occurs. This incongruence has two main results. It can exaggerate trade between countries, leading to anti-trade sentiment, and it can generate policies that do not reflect the pace, direction and reality of world production and trade. Having an accurate, evidence-based methodology of the true value of trade is necessary if policy makers are to make informed decisions on trade and economic policy.

All that is very well, you might say, but what we are seeing is job cutting and factories closing, and not the contrary. And this is where the challenge begins for statisticians. It is much easier to count the workshops that close as a result of foreign competition than those that expand their activities thanks to the efficiency linked to subcontracting; and as the accountants tell us, what cannot be counted does not count . . .

Getting the figures right

I realized several years ago that the trade negotiations being carried out at the WTO – negotiations aimed at modernizing international rules to better reflect the realities of the twenty-first century – were really still based on a nineteenth-century view of international commerce. This has certainly had something to do with the difficulties that negotiators have had – and are having – in bringing the Doha Round to a successful conclusion. But international statistical conventions take years to change and we could not wait. This is why I asked the statisticians at the WTO to find a way of bridging this gap with the necessary statistical tools. Since then, the 2008–2009 global financial crisis and the accompanying 'Great Trade Collapse' have concentrated the attention of analysts on the importance of this issue.

Statisticians essentially needed to reinvent the system of national accounting to take account of industrial interaction between the different areas of the world. The basic idea is simple and dates back to the work of Nobel laureate Wassili Leontief in the 1960s: you create a giant international input–output matrix to describe all inter-industry trade preceding production and consumption of a final good or service. The idea may be simple, but putting it into practice is complicated.

Without going into specifics, the implementation of such a tool requires not only proper harmonization of each of the partners' national accounts, but also a detailed analysis of the use of the goods and services traded, either for consumption or investment purposes or for further use in a new productive process. The latter case is, of course, crucial because it is indicative of international trade in the context of value chains: you import an intermediate product – whether a good or a service – to which you add value before re-exporting it or using it domestically, whether for consumption or for incorporation in a new productive process.

Knowledge of the value-added content of exports provides a means of avoiding double counting when intermediate components cross several borders before reaching their final destination. It also makes it possible to ascertain the portion of commercial value recorded at each customs point that is attributable to the exporting country – namely the processing of imported inputs – and what constitutes re-exportation of foreign components. Furthermore, this value addition can be further broken down between the own assets of the industry directly responsible for the exports and the indirect value-added contributions attributable to the domestic suppliers of the enterprise concerned.

Japan's Ministry of Trade and Industry had already done some pioneer work on inter-industry trade in South-East Asia, which had been supplemented by what is known as the World Input-Output Database (WIOD) initiative, a European project co-ordinated by the University of Groningen in the Netherlands. Thanks to this project, major statistical advances were made. The WTO teamed up with the OECD to initiate co-operation in further statistical and analytical work. By late 2012, this work on the methodology had made enough progress for the OECD and the WTO jointly to decide to make available to the general public a database of international trade measured in terms of value added.

Services are no longer the poor trade relation

What do the new trade figures tell us? First of all, they provide a map of international trade that vastly differs from the previous one. Let's take the example of services. Services are often described as the poor relation of globalization: even agriculture, which accounts for 7 per cent of international trade, receives closer consideration. And yet, take a look at where value added in international trade comes from today and you will frequently find a services provider. In fact, services are at the very heart of value chains, whether national or international, because the provision of industrial or commercial services, such as information technology (IT) and factoring, marketing, logistics, assembly and distribution, after-sales service and so forth, is often subcontracted.

It is therefore not surprising that the share of services more than doubles when trade is measured in value-added terms. The figures for 2008, immediately before the crisis, show a rise from 23 per cent of total trade, measured in the traditional way, to 45 per cent if one incorporates the direct and indirect value added ascribed to services. According to these new figures, services are thus the chief contributors to global trade, while manufacturing industry's share declines in the same proportion (from 65 per cent to 37 per cent).

These results have far-reaching implications for all international trade analysts, and hence for negotiators. The first lesson is that performance of the export sector, which is often reduced to a few mega-industries in key sectors such as the pharmaceutical, aeronautical and automotive sectors, in fact involves a great many more actors than might be imagined, through the network of these mega-firms' suppliers and subcontractors. This network serves a large number of small and medium-sized enterprises in all sectors of activity. The contribution of services to value added in industrial exports is particularly significant in developed countries. This is good news for employment, because, as we all know, the greatest number of jobs is generated by these services sectors. This is also an important signal for the industrialized countries as regards their comparative advantages in relation to emerging countries. It is the excellence and competitiveness of the services they supply that enable developed countries to maintain a competitive advantage over emerging ones – and here I naturally include research and development as well as management, logistics and distribution activities.

The second lesson is that to be able to export, you must know how to import. When an industry's competitiveness relies on the cost effectiveness of the components and intermediate goods and services making up the production chain, strong performance in all segments of the value chain is essential. Indeed, there is a positive correlation between the buoyancy of a country's exports and its integration in value chains through imports of intermediate goods. This is especially true of the emerging economies and the Eastern European countries – as indeed it is of industrial giants like Germany. Importing competitive components where necessary enables developed-country firms to generate margins for investing in those segments where their real comparative advantages lie. Far from killing jobs, this enables Europe, the United States and Japan to maintain industrial activities linked in particular to research and development, industrial engineering and high value-added services. These are the activities that generate the best-paid jobs.

I would even go a step further. Agreeing to import a part of the value chain from emerging countries promotes the development of a new middle class in these countries that will provide a new market for advanced economies' exports. I am convinced that the new statistics by the WTO and OECD will allow a better appreciation of this global interdependence represented by the value chains, which in turn will foster a more co-operative – I would say less mercantilist – approach to trade negotiations.

Revising trade gaps

Over the years, I have had many conversations – I could say frustrating conversations – with many members of the Committee of Ways and Means of the US House of Representatives. For many Committee members, every dollar of Chinese goods imported into the United States is a dollar stolen from an American worker or an American farmer. But standing in almost any exporting plant in China, or in any other developing country exporter of manufactured goods, such as Mexico, South Korea or Thailand, you realize just how important it is to understand how trade works in today's world and why some of these perceptions may simply be wrong.

Measuring trade in terms of value added makes it possible to reassess the problem of trade imbalances, which have been a source of increasing tension since the 2008–2009 crisis. Traditional statistics attribute the full commercial

31

value of imports to the last link in the production chain, even where the contribution made by that final link has been minimal. Knowing that the last link is often China and the importer is often the United States, the geopolitical implications of this measurement error are immediately plain to see.

But when trade is measured on the basis of the actual contribution of each country to its exports, the trade imbalance between China and the United States is reduced by more than 25 per cent. The difference is transferred to the United States' bilateral deficit with South Korea or Japan, which export components to China for assembly. The overall US deficit does not change but the geopolitical implications do. These changes are not limited to China. Germany and France, for example, export more to the United States than their traditional trade balance appears to show. This is because part of the European exports transit through other countries (China, Canada or Mexico) for processing and re-export to the United States.

This example usefully shows how the statistical bias created by attributing the full commercial value to the last country of origin can pervert the political debate – and not just in the US Ways and Means Committee – on the origin of the imbalances and lead to misguided, and hence counterproductive, decisions. It was important to reformulate traditional statistics. I am confident that this innovation – the outcome of a global co-operative endeavour – will be a milestone. And I am happy that the WTO was the driving force behind this breakthrough. All regulators know that their greatest asset is in-depth understanding of the activities they are called upon to regulate.

However, this is but the first step along a lengthy road. We still need to include a larger number of countries – especially developing countries – in the OECD-WTO database. But I assume that this new information will spark the curiosity and imagination of economists and negotiators. Thanks to this work, analysts now have better statistical tools for testing their theories and coming up with new ones. We know that there is no absolute scientific truth, especially in the economic and social spheres. However, taking the old saying about the cup being half full or half empty, if there is no absolute truth there are no big lies either. Quoting Disraeli, Mark Twain said 'there are three types of lie: lies, damn lies and statistics'. The initiative on value added has ensured that trade statistics are somewhat less of a lie. Thanks to international co-operation, we can harbour the hope that they will lie even less in the future.

Non-tariff measures

Global trade is also changing in terms of the obstacles it faces. Tariffs and non-tariff contingency measures, including anti-dumping duties and safeguards, traditionally formed the principal barrier to trade. They were the focus of international trade negotiations. But in recent years, so-called non-tariff measures (NTMs), such as technical standards, health and safety requirements and services regulations, have loomed ever larger. With the expansion of global production sharing, product and process standards are becoming increasingly relevant in linking various stages of global value chains. Quality concerns take a more central role in policy as economies develop and become more interdependent, and as incomes grow. Today, non-tariff measures are more prevalent in the richer countries but the trend is present in practically every economy. These concerns over standards are wholly legitimate and cannot, indeed should not, be blindly trumped by a desire to keep trade completely unobstructed.

That said, the nature of the measures taken to pursue public policy objectives in health and other areas, and the way these measures are administered, can have widely varying effects on trade, both positive and negative. We can agree that it is desirable to ensure that NTMs do not increase trade costs more than the minimum necessary to achieve their objective. Similarly, it is reasonable to argue that NTMs should not be constructed in ways that unduly favour domestic interests. Yet, in light of the complex objectives and policies in play where NTMs are concerned, finding the right balance is not easy. It requires co-operation and dialogue.

Our understanding of the trade effects of public policies is complicated by four factors.

First, the effect of technical measures, such as those covered by the WTO agreements on sanitary and phytosanitary measures (SPS) and on technical barriers to trade (TBT), depends significantly on how they are applied, or administered. Evidence from business surveys shows that procedural obstacles, for instance conformity assessment procedures, can be a major source of difficulties for exporting firms. Second, while public policies need not be trade distorting or trade restricting in and of themselves, they may be designed in such a way as to impart an intentionally protectionist effect, while serving a public policy objective. Such measures assume a 'dual purpose', and this interface between public policy and protectionism poses an important challenge for the WTO and has been at the heart of a growing number of trade disputes. Third, even in the absence of protectionist intent, national policies that result in regulatory discrepancies can substantially raise trade costs and reduce or distort trade flows. There are various reasons why national policies may diverge. Different regulatory approaches may not be intentional, but rather rooted in habit or custom. Divergence between national or regional public policies may also reflect different social preferences. In other words, value systems among societies may vary, giving rise to contrasts in approaches that can be difficult to reconcile.

While it can be argued without too much controversy that it is desirable to reduce the deadweight costs of inefficient systems, or to address protectionist measures hidden behind legitimate public policy interventions, it is by no means obvious that we can argue for uniformity in the substantive objectives behind public policy, even if differences impact trade. Here, the challenge is more nuanced. We would like to minimize incidental divergence, but trade can hardly trump social preferences in matters of public policy. In these circumstances – where genuine differences prevail in public preferences and objectives – regulatory harmonization or mutual recognition arrangements may be a better avenue. But what is clear is that greater political energy is necessary to reduce these divergences in order to level the playing field.

The fourth reason why NTMs can be difficult to gauge in terms of their trade impact relates to measurability. With tariffs, it is a relatively straightforward matter to estimate trade impact. NTMs are much harder to assess in these terms. But we can start by improving transparency about existing NTMs. During my tenure at the WTO, I launched the Integrated Trade Intelligence Portal (I-TIP), a one-stop shop for accessing all information notified to the WTO by members, including about NTMs, tariffs, trade remedy use and trade statistics. For the first time, it became possible to access the entire trade regime of a country.

Looking ahead, it seems to me that with NTMs we need to reflect more carefully on our core culture and approach to trade opening. A new horizon and context must be defined. With tariffs and quotas, the long-term objective of negotiations has been the progressive reduction or elimination of measures. Public policies, such as health, cannot simply be reduced and eliminated. This re-orientation in our thinking is a basic challenge. In an era where public policies move centre stage in trade politics, the objective of trade opening, and the pursuit of opportunities stemming from specialization through trade, require a clear understanding of how, when and where regulatory convergence should be promoted. This a point that will be further developed in the following chapters.

3

Helping the poorest up the prosperity ladder

When in 2000 world leaders adopted the Millennium Declaration and its eight Millennium Development Goals (MDGs), they committed themselves to an unprecedented effort to tackle global poverty. The goals, with their 21 targets for development and 60 indicators for measuring progress on halving the incidence of extreme poverty by 2015, became the blueprint for global action to address the development needs of the world's poorest countries. By creating a stable multilateral trading system, the WTO is at the forefront of efforts to forge an international environment that helps countries to grow and to reduce poverty. It is not surprising, then, that international trade – and by extension the work of the WTO – appears in the MDGs. Trade falls mainly within the targets set in the eighth MDG, which calls for the development of a global partnership for development.

The eighth MDG urges the international community to 'develop further an open, rule-based, predictable, non-discriminatory trading and financial system'. This system should ensure 'developing countries gain greater access to the markets of developed countries' and that 'least developed countries benefit most from tariff reductions, especially on their agricultural products'. By setting these targets, the international community recognized global trade as an important engine for development and showed awareness of the conditions under which international trade must operate to deliver real economic growth effectively. This closely corresponds to the WTO's central business of regulating international trade, reducing market access barriers and ensuring a more level playing field for all its members. Furthermore, in keeping with the second target, which addresses the special needs of the least-developed countries (LDCs), the WTO is committed to working towards enhancing the benefits of trade for the poorest of its members.

There is a direct correlation between integration into the multilateral trading system and economic growth, and between growth and poverty reduction. We need look no further than China, where more than 600 million people, significantly more than the population of the European Union, have been lifted out of poverty in less than thirty years. No country has achieved the sustained high growth necessary for mass poverty reduction without successfully exporting a diverse range of products into global markets. Economic growth is, of course, not the same thing as development, which is a multi-faceted process. But economic growth is an essential precondition for development to take place. The market access opportunities that international trade can provide, when accompanied by appropriate domestic policies, can ensure that international trade helps to create jobs, leads to enhanced levels of growth, improves living standards and helps countries achieve their social and developmental objectives.

In his book *Development as Freedom*, Nobel economics laureate Amartya Sen defines development as a process that expands human freedom and removes those 'unfreedoms' that leave people with little choice and few opportunities. International trade is recognized as a tool for generating opportunities for development. The WTO does not advocate open trade for its own sake, but as a means for achieving Sen's vision, enshrined in the preamble of the WTO Agreement, of 'raising standards of living, ensuring full employment and a large and steadily growing volume of real income and effective demand'.

Trade has been a vehicle for prosperity in many parts of the globe. By promoting economic growth and higher incomes, and by offering access to better goods, services, capital, knowledge and technology, trade offers new and diverse opportunities for all. What Professor Sen teaches us is that to ensure that trade opening works for the poor, trade reforms need to be accompanied by policies that guarantee an equitable distribution of trade gains. Health and education, social safety nets and access to credit are as much a part of poverty reduction strategies as economic growth itself. These complementary policies protect the poor against the potentially destabilizing effects of trade opening, while ensuring that trade unlocks income-generating potential for all layers of society. This requires overall co-ordination between government institutions as well as multilaterally through international co-operation.

How has the contribution of international trade to the development of the poorer countries progressed over the past decade and what more needs to be done? When it comes to the contribution of international trade to the performance of the LDCs, progress is unquestionable: their average growth rate of 6 per cent over the past decade is double the world average and trade accounts for two-thirds of that growth. During the same period, LDC trade grew 1.6 times as fast as world trade. In this, they have been helped by a significant rise in official development assistance (ODA) for trade capacity building, which more than doubled to US$ 13 billion in 2010 from some US$ 6 billion in the early 2000s. ODA refers to those flows provided by official agencies that have the economic development and welfare of developing countries as their main objective.

While we should be encouraged by these positive trends, they should not blind us to the challenges ahead. The total share of all LDCs in world trade may have doubled, but it is still only around 1 per cent. And this share is highly concentrated on a narrow range of commodities and raw materials. In other words, the contribution of international trade to the development of the LDCs remains inadequate and much more needs to be done.

But before discussing what the international community and the WTO should be doing, let us take a brief look at the impact that the changes in the structure of global trade we discussed in Chapter 2 are having on poorer countries. Particularly for smaller developing countries, but also for small and medium-sized companies generally, global value chains are good news. Why? Because they lower the bar for entry into the global economy as countries and companies do not need to have a full-fledged vertically integrated industry, as the example of the Samoan wire harnesses shows.

But the rise of global value chains also requires governments to rethink how best to pursue trade-led growth. Government policies can help create a virtuous circle of increasing international competitiveness and trade flows, yielding steady development dividends. Public–private co-operation can encourage foreign direct investment, which often brings with it better technology. Investments in infrastructure, coupled with efficient business and support services, can help deepen ties between countries, making it easier to fragment production regionally. Reduced transaction costs boost the competitiveness of domestic firms.

What can the multilateral trading system do to smooth the path of LDCs through the world economy? How can we encourage the development of new trade flows? And how can developing countries be helped up the value chain to create more growth and jobs? One clear way would be to complete the Doha Development Agenda (DDA), the official name of the WTO round of trading opening negotiations.

The Doha Round was launched in November 2001 in the aftermath of the 11 September attacks on the United States, which had created a new element of economic uncertainty. In launching it, WTO members put development issues at the heart of the new negotiations. The Uruguay Round, the last multilateral trade round to be completed, wrote the modern rulebook for the trading system. The Doha Round aims to use this book to open trade further and lock in reforms on an unprecedented scale. A fundamental aspect of the DDA is to address some of the imbalances in trade rules that have restricted the ability of developing countries to export.

The Round is deadlocked for reasons that are discussed in Chapter 13. It is a pity because I have no hesitation in saying that, going by what is on the table of the negotiations so far, significant export opportunities would arise for developing countries – in agriculture, industrial tariffs and services.

The conclusion of the Doha Round would also realize a long-standing aspiration of LDCs: duty-free, quota-free market access for their exports. Most developed country members of the WTO, and the United States is one of the exceptions, have already met the target of providing duty-free, quota-free market access to 97 per cent of products originating from LDCs, agreed by trade ministers in 2005. A number of leading developing countries, including China, India, South Korea and Turkey, are doing the same, and others are actively looking into taking similar measures. So this is an area where the richer developing countries are already taking on more responsibility when it comes to helping the poorest.

I know how hard it is to convince your domestic constituencies to open their market to imports, even if they come from the poorest countries on earth. Some will say that exporters from these countries do not respect Western standards; others will say that providing the same opportunities to all LDCs will, in effect, be to the detriment of some of the weaker among them, as levels of poverty may be greater in Africa than in Asia or vice versa; still others will say it's about aid and not trade.

I had to face many of these arguments as I crafted the European Union's duty-free and quota-free scheme for LDCs – the 'Everything but Arms' initiative, which earned me undisguised dislike from some European leaders eager to protect their sugar or rice lobbies.

However, we need to remain faithful to the promise we made at the UN LDCs Conference in 2001 to open our markets fully to the world's poorest. We have seen how this opportunity can translate into growth, development and jobs on the ground. It is not about providing opportunities to poor countries at the expense of domestic jobs. It is often about refusing to protect uncompetitive domestic producers at the expense of citizens living below the poverty line of US$ 2 a day. It's also not about putting trade ahead of any other social consideration. With trade opening comes empowerment, and with it, accountability. It is probably a better avenue to ensure that respecting higher standards within countries becomes a domestic issue, as we have recently seen in Bangladesh.

Removing obstacles to trade, however, is often not enough for countries to reap the benefits of trade opening, including the ones that will come as a result of a successful conclusion of the DDA. To fully benefit from further trade opening, countries require the right domestic policies, institutional capacity and economic infrastructure. This is as true in developed countries as it is in developing countries. The difference is that developed countries are able to mobilize the needed resources and their businesses have the capacity to pursue and exploit fully the opportunities presented by trade opening.

Making trade opening work for the poor

At the ministerial conference in Hong Kong in 2005, my first as WTO chief, trade ministers gave the WTO a mandate to help co-ordinate developing countries, especially the least developed, in building the trade capacity they need to take advantage of new trading opportunities. The initiative, known as Aid for Trade, provides financial and technical assistance to poorer countries so that they can 'produce more and trade better'. It aims to help them develop the competitive, well-regulated logistics and services sectors that can be as important as physical infrastructure to trade competitiveness. It also assists developing country producers in upgrading equipment, improving marketing activities and complying with international standards and other non-tariff requirements, helping them move up value chains. It also helps developing countries to adjust to the changes led by greater trade opening. The initiative was something that I had pushed for hard, because I firmly believed, after my years as EU Trade Commissioner, that it was needed if all countries were to benefit from a more open trading system. Aid for Trade is the bridge between trade and development. The initiative achieved widespread ministerial support in Hong Kong, in particular from the Republican US Trade Representative, Rob Portman, who announced that the United States would double its contribution to Aid for Trade – from USD 1.3 billion in 2005 to USD 2.7 billion annually by 2010 – as well as from the EU Trade Commissioner, Peter Mandelson.

The work, spearheaded by the WTO in partnership with the OECD, the World Bank, regional development banks and UN agencies, has helped to mobilize substantial resources. In 2010, US$ 45 billion in Aid for Trade was committed to developing countries, with an increasing amount going to least-developed and low-income countries in Africa and Asia, which took 30 per cent and 16 per cent, respectively. But the WTO is not a development agency, and I was always clear that Aid for Trade was not about transforming the WTO into one. It was about co-ordination. It was about creating a platform for accountability. It offers a focal point to bring together the relevant actors – agencies, donors and beneficiaries. The biennial Aid for Trade Global Review, which the WTO has been hosting since 2007, provides an opportunity to look at what is being done, see where the gaps are, ensure financing is adequate and monitor the impact that policies are having on the ground. The WTO's role is to ensure the necessary policy coherence, which is a key theme of this book, and a key goal of Aid for Trade.

Assistance to LDCs under Aid for Trade is channelled through the specially created Enhanced Integrated Framework (EIF), which is a very bureaucratic name for a very effective joint endeavour by six international organizations (the IMF, the International Trade Centre, the United Nations Conference on Trade and Development (UNCTAD), the United Nations Development Programme (UNDP), the World Bank and the WTO). At the time of writing, the programme was helping forty-eight countries, supported by a multi-donor trust fund, the EIF Trust Fund, with contributions from twenty-three donors. Essentially it offers a gateway to Aid for Trade for LDCs, a platform where demand for and supply of trade-related assistance can be matched.

Another vehicle is the Standards and Trade Development Facility, which is a global partnership that helps developing countries improve their capacity to implement international sanitary and phytosanitary (SPS) standards and regulations regarding human, animal and plant health. As we discussed in Chapter 2, non-tariff barriers, which include SPS measures, can be a major obstacle to poorer countries accessing new markets. The Facility was set up by the UN Food and Agriculture Organization (FAO), the World Organisation for Animal Health (OIE), the World Bank, the

World Health Organization (WHO) and the WTO, which houses its secretariat. It is financed by voluntary contributions and is another example of policy coherence in action.

Export growth is necessary for the benefits of more open trade to be felt. For exports to grow, entrepreneurs need adequate and credible information about policy changes, both domestic and international, and adequate information about possible export markets, and they need to be able to make the investments necessary to expand or start exporting. Often these conditions are not satisfied in developing countries. In Tanzania, for instance, less than 10 per cent of the population has access to the formal banking sector. This represents a formidable difficulty in mobilizing the entrepreneurial potential that may be available in the population.

But even if they have the necessary information and financial support, there are a host of other factors that will affect whether entrepreneurs are able to get their products to market in good time and at a good price; in other words, whether they will have products capable of competing on global markets. For trade to flourish, and for companies and entrepreneurs to be competitive, transport systems have to be efficient, which in turn requires good roads, rail connections, ports and airports. But more than this is needed. There also have to be efficient and transparent customs procedures and border controls, with clear rules and regulations covering customs fees and duties. All these things facilitate trade. It is simple mathematics. If the cost of exporting from or importing into one country is more expensive than in another, then – all other things being equal – the first country will be less competitive, less attractive to investment and will find it more difficult to move up the value chain. There are many poorer developing countries where hardly any of these necessary conditions for trading competitively exist.

The Aid for Trade initiative reflected an important, and some may say, seismic shift in how WTO countries approached trade negotiations. It does not propose wrapping poorer developing countries in a protective blanket of exceptions and exclusions from the open trade commitments undertaken by their richer partners, which was the earlier approach. Rather, it aims to empower poor developing countries in attaining a level of economic development that will permit them, in time, to undertake these same commitments. It emphasizes creating capacity rather than creating get-out clauses. This is why I believe Aid for Trade must be an integral part of the WTO now. It is why I believe it is disingenuous to consider this initiative as extraneous to the WTO, as it cannot be dissociated from the WTO's core function of opening trade. The rumblings of this change in approach were already felt with the launch of WTO negotiations on a trade facilitation agreement, which aims at cutting the red tape that too often hampers trade. A multilateral agreement – which appeared close at the time of writing – would expedite the movement of goods across borders, by, for example, simplifying customs procedures, and improve the transparency and predictability of trade. The agreement would recognize – for the first time – an explicit link between adopting WTO commitments and the technical assistance needed to implement them. This is a huge step forward in the traditional design of WTO agreements.

For governments and especially for the private sector, the buzzwords are 'quicker, easier and less costly' when it comes to looking at competitiveness. And I am yet to find a government or business that does not have competitiveness at the core of its development or business strategy. With the growing prevalence of regional and global supply chains, effective and predictable trading across borders is an essential ingredient in making supply chains work for developing countries.

The port of Chittagong is the busy import–export and transit hub of Bangladesh. It is a port that has had its problems. Not so many years ago, the Asian Development Bank decried its 'over-staffing, labour strikes, cumbersome customs procedures, out-dated and inefficient work rules, out-dated and inflexible management'. But today, behind the traditional bustle of ships loading and unloading goods and bills of entry trading hands, a quiet electronic revolution of trade transactions and customs clearance is taking place. On a visit in early 2013, I saw goods being cleared without the need of reams of signatures, cargo scanned in an efficient way and, more importantly, imports being cleared with an urgency that confirmed that facilitating trade is as important for this LDC as for the United States or for any country in Europe.

The total cost of trading across borders is estimated at US$ 2 trillion dollars a year – some 10 per cent of the value of global trade. Globally, reducing these barriers to trade by cutting red tape in half, which is what a multilateral trade facilitation agreement could deliver, could stimulate the US$ 22 trillion dollar world economy by more than US$ 1 trillion dollars. In terms of boosting the global economy, this could be the equivalent of removing all tariffs worldwide, which today stand at around 5 per cent. The income-creating impact of that is further multiplied for goods and services in regional and global value chains that may have to cross borders several times in their production and distribution cycle. It could also be particularly beneficial to poor landlocked developing countries, such as Laos, Nepal, Rwanda, Paraguay or Zambia, for whom trade nearly always involves crossing more than one frontier.

Outcomes matter. It matters whether we are achieving the Millennium Development Goals. It matters whether an economic project has an impact on social development and vice versa. It matters that we can use evidence to decide where to allocate scarce Aid for Trade resources. With budgets around the world tightening, the allocation of resources based on objective and impact will increasingly drive policy decisions. To ensure that these decisions can be accurate and effective, evidence – both quantitatively robust and qualitatively rich – must serve as the central arbitrator.

Annualized over the period 2005–2011, the volume of world merchandise trade grew by some 3.7 per cent annually – albeit with a sharp downturn in 2009. For many developing countries, growth rates over this period were much higher. For example, LDCs' merchandise exports grew by 4.6 per cent a year. By contributing to mobilizing the potential of developing countries to participate in world trade, Aid for Trade can reasonably claim to have played a part in this expansion. Take the case of Rwanda, where the European Union has been supporting coffee and tea export projects. By 2009, the EU programme had contributed to a 38 per cent rise in the total export value for coffee and tea. The share of fully washed coffee, which yields better quality, had increased from zero to 24 per cent, while productivity in the tea sector had risen to 7 tonnes of leaves per hectare from 5.7 tonnes previously.

But concentrating on just the numerical outcomes is perhaps too limiting a focus. This is fundamentally because the Aid for Trade initiative is first and foremost about winning the argument on mainstreaming trade in national development strategies. What does that mean? It means ensuring that when development policy agendas and strategies are being drawn up, for example for meeting the MDGs, trade is on that agenda, it is one of the items for which strategies will be developed. Aid for Trade is also about helping countries and the decision makers and policy makers (and policy takers) see the wisdom of making trade a development policy priority.

Trade finance: a major obstacle

It is also about trade finance, its affordability and accessibility. Trade finance is a crucial factor in the trade and development equation. Between 80 and 90 per cent of world trade relies on commercial financing, mostly of a short-term nature. But only a third of the poorest countries benefit regularly from the services offered by trade finance programmes. And even where trade finance is available, it does not mean that access is universal. In practice, access varies significantly, both between countries and within countries. Least-developed countries in Africa and Asia typically fare the worst, although they are not alone. Small and medium-sized enterprises (SMEs) face serious challenges in many places. In short, there are a series of 'structural access' issues that affect the market for trade finance. The worry is that a lack of well-functioning trade finance markets could be a more important barrier to trade, in particular for low-income countries, than traditional obstacles, such as high tariff barriers.

The fastest growing market for trade finance is suppliers' credit. Trade finance follows the patterns of global trade. It should not come as a surprise, therefore, that the vast majority of trade finance operations cover trade in intermediate products – the inputs and parts that constitute consumer goods. The heavy volume of transactions which intermediate trade needs has led suppliers and their banks to change their modus operandi. Open account formats, whereby liquidity is granted against proof of order, contract or bills of exchange, are becoming the norm in trade finance. Existing instruments like letters of credit are still used but are less adapted to the high volume of orders and deliveries generated by geographically fragmented value chains.

Where banks and their exporter customers lack adequate collateral, markets lose confidence. In the absence of confidence, one of two outcomes occurs: a high level of risk is priced into transactions, making them unaffordable to all but a few, or no price is offered at all. The conundrum of trade finance is that it is one of the safest forms of finance around. Research by the International Chamber of Commerce, the International Finance Corporation and others has shown that defaults are very infrequent. Of course, when the spectre of global financial crisis enters the frame, as it did in 2008, collateral and confidence issues can get badly misaligned. The credit crunch that grew out of the financial crisis also drove liquidity out of the trade finance market, and it risked amplifying the downturn in global trade experienced in 2009.

At the WTO we were able to galvanize some action on these issues. In early 2009 we dusted off the 'Expert Group on Trade Finance' – a forum to encourage greater transparency, dialogue and information sharing among export credit agencies, commercial banks and the multilateral and regional financial institutions. It had been around for a while but little used. However, with G20 leaders due to gather in London in April for the second time on the global economic crisis, it seemed the ideal body to provide the insights and information needed to press the summit to act on trade financing. At the meeting, World Bank chief Bob Zoellick and I, with the support of many heads of states, successfully argued in favour of a package of up to US$ 250 billion in additional short-term trade finance and guarantees to be mobilized in two years by public-backed institutions.

This package helped restore confidence in markets relatively rapidly, to a large extent due to the mobilization of export credit agencies and multilateral financial institutions. Within a year of implementation, the initiative helped mobilize US$ 170 billion in additional support to underwrite trade transactions. But just as important has been our less high-profile advocacy work in other areas, such as with the Basel Committee on Banking Supervision, which seeks to set guidelines and standards for commercial banks to ensure that rules governing trade finance are commensurate with a low-risk profile.

For trade finance markets to operate efficiently, sound monetary and banking policies, transparent fiscal and financial regimes, and functioning capital and insurance markets need to be in place – as well as the necessary legal and regulatory frameworks to encourage domestic and foreign investment. That way, collateral is ensured and confidence maintained. Aid for Trade can play a catalytic role by helping tackle issues of access. But trade finance is a commercial activity, and while Aid for Trade can help address market failure, it cannot, nor should it, be a substitute for the commercial character of the market. One of the challenges that we face is to ensure that while helping to overcome access issues, we do not at the same time crowd out the very private sector actors we need to make markets work effectively.

One other thing that the work of the WTO Expert Group made clear was that trade finance transactions in sub-Saharan Africa had declined dramatically – beyond what could be explained by the contraction of trade flows – and beyond what was being experienced in other regions with developing countries. Regional development banks, such as the Asian Development Bank, the Inter-American Development Bank or the European Bank for Reconstruction and Development, provide a large part of trade finance for what is perceived as the low end of the market. They do this through trade facilitation programmes, which either guarantee operations of the private sector or act as intermediaries directly in the market. The one regional bank that did not have such a facility was the African Development Bank (ADB).

In early 2013, at the request of ADB President Donald Kaberuka, a brilliant and charismatic Rwandan, I went to Tunis to address the bank's board and impress on them the importance of trade finance for SMEs in Africa. Now a facilitation programme might seem an obvious weapon for a regional development bank to have in its armoury, but some would argue that money spent on guaranteeing trade finance is not money available for health, education and other policy priorities. My message was simple: there were huge sections of the African economy that would continue with no access to the financing they needed to trade unless the ADB stepped in and helped. Given its self-financing nature, it need not reduce funds for other priorities. In February 2013, the board agreed to set up just such a facility.

Some have praised trade opening as the 'most powerful' and 'life-enhancing' force on earth. Such praise could give the impression that the WTO is in the business of creating 'magic potions', which, if taken, automatically stimulate growth and create jobs around the globe. But some sixty years of multilateral trade negotiations have taught us that WTO potions are not magic. They are just like any medicine on offer in pharmacies: they do not always have the same effect on everybody and they can sometimes have side effects.

But no medicines are of use if they do not find their way to the patients.

Market-access or market-opening commitments made by WTO members during multilateral trade negotiations may turn out to be of little or no use to poor WTO members, which, because of internal capacity constraints, such as inadequate infrastructure, may be unable to take advantage of the new trading opportunities on offer. This is why Aid for Trade is so important. And effective trade assistance requires effective policy coherence both between international actors and with domestic policy makers.

4

Trade: friend not foe of the environment

In June 2008, to coincide with the trade ministers' conference being held in Geneva, a non-governmental organization (NGO) called Oceana plastered the city with posters bearing the words 'WTO, please save our fish'. They were asking for the WTO's help in resolving the damaging environmental problem of overfishing. What a sea change from the views many NGOs expressed – sometimes violently – at a similar ministerial conference in Seattle in 1999. There the WTO, with its advocacy of open trade, was accused of abetting the wholesale 'murder' of dolphins and turtles. In just a few years the WTO had moved from being the villain of the hour, when it came to environmental protection, to a potential saviour. It had become a place where activists believed that the environment could be defended, where fish could be protected.

This is a far fairer view because, contrary to the lingering perception of some, trade can be a friend, and not a foe, of conservation. Trade opening has much to contribute in the protection of the environment and the fight against climate change. The founding fathers of the organization were adamant that sustainable development must lie at the very core of its mission, because only then would trade enhance human welfare. Sustainable development that 'protects and preserves' the environment is enshrined as a goal in the opening paragraph of the Marrakesh Agreement of 1994 that gave birth to the WTO. And there is no bigger challenge to sustainable development today than climate change.

Trade can allow for a more efficient allocation of all resources, including natural resources. Trade opening can help countries with scarce water resources save their precious reserves by purchasing water-intensive food products from others. As we have seen, trade generates economic growth, which in turn can create demand for higher environmental standards together with the financial capacity to respond to this demand. But we must also remember that we inhabit a world where millions continue to live on less than US$ 1 dollar a day. This has direct implications for sustainable development. Some twenty-five years have passed since the publication of the report by the World Commission on Environment and Development, better known as the Brundtland Report, but its conclusions remain valid. Many countries still face what it called the 'pollution of poverty'. Poverty forces people to over-exploit their natural environment, and such over-exploitation, in turn, hurts their chances of development, for a healthy natural resource base is itself a vital ingredient for economic growth.

But the capacity of markets to deliver efficient outcomes is linked to what we place within the market. As we saw in Chapter 3, the WTO has the capacity to open borders – and thereby to switch on an important engine of economic growth – but for the benefits of that growth to show, countries need 'accompanying policies', whether economic, social or political. On the environmental side, honouring international accords on environmental issues is a fundamental part of such accompanying policies. The WTO must ensure that its rules do not frustrate the implementation of multilateral accords on protecting the environment (MEAs). The WTO must support these accords and strengthen the consensus on which they are based. Countries need to ensure that trade – which has the capacity to help the environment – does not end up doing the opposite. Trade in dangerous materials, such as hazardous wastes and unsafe chemicals, for example, may increase environmental and occupational health hazards, especially in developing countries, if appropriate handling or disposal cannot be guaranteed.

The WTO must also ensure that its own rules help to correct environmental problems, whether they be over-fishing, fossil fuel subsidies or state agricultural subsidies that can end up doing environmental damage. The billions of dollars in subsidies poured into fishing fleets have encouraged 'too many fishermen to chase after too few fish', resulting in the depletion of the world's oceans. The Doha Round represents the first time environmental issues, including fishing, are included in multilateral trade negotiations. The negotiations on the environment have three distinct 'chapters', each with its unique contribution to make to a greener global economy.

Greener goods

First, the Round calls for accelerating trade opening for environmentally friendly technologies, such as enhanced access to the windmills and solar panels that would make for a greener energy future. More open trade should increase the availability and lower the cost of environmentally friendly goods, services and technologies. This is particularly important for countries that do not have access to them or whose domestic industries do not produce them in sufficient scale or at affordable prices. For exporters, additional market access can provide incentives to develop environmentally friendly new products. So the negotiations on environmental goods and services could deliver a double win: a win for the environment and a win for trade.

Economists tell us that the global market for environmental goods and services is estimated to be worth more than US\$ 550 billion dollars a year. The OECD estimates that green services account for 65 per cent of this market and green goods 35 per cent. For a country such as Indonesia, which is among the world's top ten exporters of steam condensers, the negotiations can represent just such a double win. The same goes for India, which is among the world's top ten exporters of hydraulic turbines, for Malaysia, which is among the world's top five exporters of photovoltaic cells or for Thailand, which ranks among the top ten exporters of filtering and purifying machinery for gases.

It would be unfortunate to miss an opportunity to open markets for clean technology and services. However, we should also be aware of the fact that, ultimately, it is the existence of environmental regulations that will drive demand for environmental goods and services. Hence the importance of setting the right environmental framework within which market opening can take place. Trade cannot do it alone; it requires effective and coherent international environmental policies.

Second, the Doha negotiations demand that WTO rules and multilateral environmental agreements be mutually supportive. There are some 200 MEAs, ranging from limits on the use of ozone-depleting substances to combating desertification and protecting endangered species, and at least 10 of them contain provisions relating to trade. The WTO has long debated how to strengthen compatibility between WTO rules and such treaties so that whatever is agreed in a multilateral environmental negotiation is not overturned later by the WTO. The WTO's Appellate Body – its top trade court – went a long way towards creating this greater certainty when it decreed that trade rules cannot be interpreted in 'clinical isolation' and must take into account other international agreements. In fact, the WTO has never overturned a trade measure mandated in an MEA and the Appellate Body has frequently taken into account the legal provisions of MEAs when resolving trade disputes between WTO members.

Third, the Doha Round aims to reduce or eliminate environmentally harmful fisheries subsidies. Today, we run the risk that overfishing will so deplete fish stocks in our oceans that many species will disappear forever. This is not only bad news for the oceans; it is bad news for the world's 43.5 million full-time fishers. Governments have contributed to this problem by providing nearly US$ 16 billion annually in subsidies to the fisheries sector. This support keeps more boats on the water and fewer fish in the sea.

While trade opening can support the green economy, the WTO also serves to keep green protectionism in check. The WTO rulebook is designed to allow WTO members to pursue legitimate environmental and sustainable development goals, providing these do not amount to arbitrary or unjustifiable discrimination against the goods of another member country, or create disguised restrictions on trade. It establishes the fine line between protection and protectionism and in so doing furthers the pursuit of legitimate societal goals.

Climate change and trade

The WTO does not have rules and regulations that are specific to climate change, but the issue intersects with international trade in a number of ways. International trade requires that goods be transported from one country to another, so expanding international trade is likely to lead to increased use of transport. And transport, most of it petroleum-fuelled, is an important source of greenhouse gases, or is it?

The scientific evidence is clear that the earth's climate system is warming as a result of greenhouse gas emissions that are still increasing and will continue to increase over the coming decades unless there are significant changes to current laws, policies and actions. Although more open trade could lead to increased CO_2 emissions as a result of rising economic activity, it can also help alleviate climate change, for instance by increasing the diffusion of technologies that mitigate the effect.

Today, there are many different perceptions of what the trading system ought to do on climate change. While some would like to see the trading system curb its own 'carbon footprint' by cutting the greenhouse gas emissions it generates in the course of the production, international transportation and consumption of traded goods and services, others would approach the issue differently by focusing on 'offsetting' measures. Offsetting essentially means taking positive action, perhaps in another geographical area, to compensate for a negative environmental impact, with the aim of leaving the overall ecological balance unchanged. There are many different ideas on what these offsetting measures might be, with most of the discussion naturally focusing on countries' most trade-exposed, energy-intensive, economic sectors, like iron and steel and aluminium.

While some are considering the imposition of domestic carbon taxes, others are contemplating emission cap-and-trade systems, with an obligation upon importers to participate. Cap-and-trade systems set limits on emissions, but give flexibility on how these limits are met. Yet another group would prefer to focus on what is most immediately 'deliverable' by the trading system in terms of the fight against climate change. And by this, they mean the opening of markets to environmental goods and services, which we have already mentioned as being part of the ongoing Doha Round.

My starting point in this debate is to say that the relationship between international trade – and indeed the WTO – and climate change, would be best defined by a consensual international accord on climate change that successfully embraced all major polluters. In other words, until a truly global consensus emerges on how best to tackle the issue of climate change, WTO members will continue to hold different views on what the multilateral trading system can and must do on this subject. Again, we need coherence when it comes to international policy.

Trade regulations are not, and cannot be, a substitute for environmental regulations. Trade, and the WTO toolbox of trade rules more specifically, can – at best – offer no more than part of the answer to climate change. It is not in the WTO that a deal on climate change can be struck, but rather in an environmental forum, such as the United Nations Framework Convention on Climate Change. Such an agreement must then send the WTO an appropriate signal on how its rules may best be put to the service of sustainable development; in other words, a signal on how its particular toolbox of rules should be employed in the fight against climate change.

Without such a signal, confusion will persist on what would constitute an appropriate response by the multilateral trading system. Let us take the issue of the international trading system's carbon footprint for instance. Much is said in the press about the carbon footprint of international transportation. We see frequent reference to the concept of 'food miles' – in other words, the desire of consumers in certain countries to calculate the carbon emitted in the course of international transportation, with many already drawing the conclusion that it may be better to 'simply produce goods at home' to minimize emissions.

Not all is what it seems

But that argument does not always stand up to empirical verification. In fact, 90 per cent of internationally traded goods are carried by sea. And maritime transport is by far the most carbon-efficient mode of transport, with only 14 grams of CO_2 emissions per ton kilometre. Shipping is followed by train transport and then road transport. Air transport has by far the highest CO_2 emissions per ton kilometre (a minimum of 600 grams), illustrating the high relative climate change impact of such transport.

However, various studies conducted on the 'carbon mileage' of traded goods have shown that the issue can often be counter-intuitive. The form of transport (air, road, maritime or rail) and distance are not the only significant contributors to CO_2 emissions. The life cycle of the products, including production methods, for example heated greenhouses versus open-air production, energy-intensive modern techniques versus hand labour, also plays a big part. Some studies show that a Kenyan flower that is air freighted to Europe emits one-third of the CO_2 of flowers grown in Holland. Others show that New Zealand lamb that is transported to the United Kingdom can actually generate 70 per cent less CO_2 than lamb produced in the UK. Similarly, some of the fertilizers produced in the United States and transported to Europe can generate 13 per cent less CO_2 than fertilizer produced in Italy. And so on.

Now, I am not saying that this will always be the case, but surely this is an issue in need of case-by-case analysis and empirical studies. For food, the cost of greenhouses in colder climates, and of energy-expensive, out-of-season storage, has to be taken into account, for example.

Only a multilateral approach to climate change would allow us to properly address these issues. Only with such an instrument can we move towards the proper pricing of energy.

Similarly, only such an accord could act as a proper arbiter of the measures that are environmentally necessary within a country. An effective multilateral solution to climate change should operate within an environmental architecture that successfully levels the playing field, based on recognized principles of international environmental law such as 'common but differentiated responsibility'. The latter recognizes the different historical contributions made by countries – mainly developed and developing – to global environmental problems and the different financial, technological and structural capacity they have to tackle them.

In working towards an international accord on climate change, countries will certainly have to reflect on the role of international trade within such an accord. As we have seen, trade leads to efficiency gains based on comparative advantage and to economic growth. But for the benefits of trade to truly materialize, for its efficiency gains to translate into fewer greenhouse gas emissions, the right environmental context must be set for trade. In other words, energy must be properly priced and production processes adjusted accordingly. It would then be incumbent upon the trading system to respond to such environmental rules as soon as they are crafted.

The WTO toolbox of rules can certainly be leveraged in the fight against climate change and 'adapted', if governments perceive this to be necessary, to better achieve their goals. The WTO has rules on product standards, for instance, that encourage its members to use the international norms set by more specialized international institutions. The WTO has rules on taxes, intellectual property (IP) and so on. All of these tools can prove valuable in the fight against climate change. But in that fight they would need to be mobilized under clear environmental parameters that only the environmental community can set.

In the absence of such parameters, the WTO will continue to be pulled from left to right by different players, with only a faint possibility of landing in the centre. Each of its members will have a different interpretation to offer on how the playing field may best be levelled. And I would caution against such an outcome; the world could end up with a real spaghetti bowl of 'offsetting' measures that achieve neither trade nor environmental goals.

There is no doubt that an immediate contribution that the WTO can make to the fight against climate change is indeed to open markets to clean technology and services, such as scrubbers, air filters and energy management services. But, as can be expected, what is and is not an environmental good is a topic that is hotly debated. At the moment, many climate adaptation and mitigation technologies are on the negotiating table. These goods and services, with an export value of some US$ 165 billion a year, include wind turbines, solar cooking appliances and photovoltaic cells. We must make this technology more accessible to all.

In recent years, however, the impressive growth rate of certain developing countries has caused a big shift in the global economy and has moved the trading system out of its equilibrium. For some, emerging economies have attained a level of development that warrants greater reciprocity of obligations, while for others, the income gap with the advanced countries renders equality of disciplines unfair. As we shall see, the inability to find a new balance in the multilateral trading system is an important barrier to concluding the Doha Round.

In many ways, reaching a meaningful agreement on a global response to climate change faces similar challenges.

The 1992 Earth Summit Declaration in Rio recognized that, even though all countries bear a responsibility to address climate change, countries have not all contributed equally to causing the problem, nor are they all equally equipped to address it. The principle of 'common but differential responsibility' was introduced in the 1997 Kyoto Protocol that established specific and binding emission reduction commitments for developed countries. Developing countries had no binding obligations.

The 2009 conference in Copenhagen represented a step forward in the bid to update Kyoto, which addressed about 30 per cent of global carbon emissions. In contrast, the framework accord hammered out in Copenhagen encompassed the majority of world emissions, but based on non-enforceable pledges rather than binding commitments. At the Durban climate summit in 2011, countries agreed to reach a new legally binding agreement encompassing all players by 2015. But we still have some way to go to achieve the sort of international agreement needed to halt the dangerous trend towards global warming.

Difficulties are inevitable when leaders confront global problems while remaining accountable largely to domestic politics. We are familiar with this in the WTO. Multilateral processes involve a great many actors and this makes reaching consensus complicated. But in the end, it is only through a multilateral process that we can achieve results that are legitimate and credible. The world is well aware of the environmental threats, but the ability of governments to respond is tied too closely to the resources at their disposal. Countries that have had success in alleviating poverty and raising living standards tend to be more adept at creating the conditions for a cleaner environment. Yet there is no doubting that the problem is one that we cannot tackle individually. Global problems require global solutions for which sound global governance – as in so many of the issues being tackled in this book – holds the key.

5

Trading towards global food security

Global food security, understood as adequate and safe supplies of food, and managing the double-edged sword of high world food prices is also an area requiring coherent international and domestic agricultural policies. While higher food prices can benefit farmers, they endanger the food security of vulnerable consumers. Remember that combating hunger and poverty is top of the UN's Millennium Development Goals (MDG). Tackling hunger and malnutrition needs better production, particularly in Africa, and requires that trade in food flows unhindered from the lands of the plenty to the lands of the less well off. Without action in these two areas, there is a risk that hunger will become even more widespread, with many million more lives at stake.

The irony is that in the 1970s Africa was a net exporter of food and such crises were far less common. Yet within twenty years, Africa had become a net food importer. The reason for this is simple: even at a time of great productivity gains globally, African agricultural production failed to keep pace with the growing population. Between 1960 and 2008, world corn production yields doubled from 2.5 tonnes to 5.0 tonnes per hectare. Yet in Africa, yields stayed stuck at under 2.0 tonnes. Milk production per cow in Africa is a quarter of the global average. It is vital to increase yields. African governments need to reassess policies that have discouraged farmers from staying on the land. Farmers should be offered incentives to use new methods and technologies. It can be done. One needs only to look at Brazil to see that African agriculture can be turned around. Just thirty years ago, Brazil was a net importer of basic foodstuffs. Today, thanks to sound policies and enhanced investment in research and development, Brazil is among the world's top exporters of wheat, corn, chicken, beef and sugar. Low levels of African agricultural productivity have kept the continent on the sidelines of global agricultural trade.

But the challenge of food security is not restricted to Africa. Many factors have been cited as causes of the repeated food crises that we have witnessed in many parts of the world in recent years. The most recent such crises were in 2008 and 2011, when the world faced severe shortages of widely consumed staples such as wheat and rice. Among the factors often mentioned are the switching of food crops to biofuel production, rising oil prices, changing diets in emerging markets, declining grain stocks, financial speculation and climate change and its associated risk. Some would add that export bans imposed in response to the 2008 crisis by some food-producing countries were themselves a cause of price hikes, in particular for commodities such as rice. In a world of nearly 200 countries, there are only between 5 and 10 major exporters of cereals. Rice, the staple food for most of humanity, is a case in point. Roughly 70 per cent of rice production comes from five countries: China, India, Indonesia, Bangladesh and Vietnam.

With production and export in the hands of so few countries, an event in any one of them that curtails the supply of grain on the market can lead to sharp spikes in prices.

In some cases, supply can be hit by floods or droughts, which lie outside the control of policy makers. But in other cases, supply declines as a direct result of policy actions, notably restrictions on exports. Governments that impose export restrictions – quotas, taxes or bans – often do so for the understandable reason that they want to ensure adequate supplies of meat or cereals for domestic consumers. As the export of agricultural products is concentrated in relatively few countries, the absence of even one big player from the export market can have a dramatic effect on prices. It was the single most important reason for the 2007–2008 price explosion on the rice market, when there was no fundamental market imbalance. Equally, the 2011 price rise for cereals had much to do with the export restrictions imposed by Russia and Ukraine after they suffered severe drought.

Food security at the heart of the WTO

Food security, which the 1996 World Food Summit defined as existing 'when all people at all times have access to sufficient, safe, nutritious food to maintain a healthy and active life', is at the heart of the WTO's mission. Its Agreement on Agriculture, which is a core part of the Uruguay Round, was the first attempt by the international community to create a level playing field in the area of agricultural trade. It disciplined the use of trade-distorting subsidies, export subsidies and tariffs, and allowed the developing world to regain some of the comparative advantage that it was previously denied. But it did not go far enough. The Doha Round remains a tremendous opportunity to carry out the additional reforms required. International trade, if properly designed and implemented, should help us escape the clutches of these repeated food crises.

But food and agricultural trade policy does not operate in a vacuum. In other words, no matter how sophisticated our trade policies may be, if domestic policies do not themselves encourage and facilitate agriculture, we will always have a problem, as we can see from Africa. Land management, water and natural resource management, property rights, storage, energy, transportation and distribution networks, credit systems, and science and technology, are all key elements of a successful agricultural policy and food security system. Take the issue of farm size. In many parts of the world, in particular in the world's poorest corners, land is being divided through inheritance amongst a growing population, and farm sizes are dwindling.

In India, the average landholding fell from 2.6 hectares in 1960 to 1.4 in 2000 and is still declining. In Bangladesh, the situation is worse. The number of farms literally doubled in this period, with farm sizes going from 1.4 to 0.6 hectares, with a rise also in landlessness. While small farms have their advantages, yields tend to be higher on larger holdings. It is also well documented that some of the world's poorest countries have taxed agriculture the most and that reinvestment of tax revenue into agriculture has been low. The policy mix at the national level, therefore, must be the starting point for any discussion of food and agricultural policy.

Trade policy cannot and does not by itself answer each and every challenge in agriculture, not least because, at the end of the day, trade is merely a transmission belt between supply and demand. It allows food-surplus countries to serve the needs of countries in food deficit. That transmission belt has to work smoothly, with as little friction as possible, but it is simply one element of a much more complex machine.

While the international community, broadly speaking, agrees on what the basic objectives of agricultural policy are, I believe that there continues to be a disagreement on what 'global integration' (in particular more open international trade) can do for agriculture. Despite the WTO Agreement on Agriculture and despite the decision to launch the Doha Round, there are still those who ask themselves, 'Is greater global integration beneficial or harmful to agriculture?' That is the question that underlies WTO negotiations in this field. Let me explain. Clearly, all agricultural policy makers want agricultural systems that provide sufficient food, feed and fibre, and that deliver nutritious food and feed. They want a decent and rising living standard for farmers. They want food to be available and affordable for the consumer. They want agricultural production systems that are in tune with local culture and customs and respect the environment throughout a product's entire life cycle. And, clearly, they would aspire to agricultural systems that are also capable of responding to the challenge of climate change.

But where the international community still disagrees is on what global integration could bring to this process. To my mind, global integration allows us to think of efficiency beyond national boundaries. It allows us to score efficiency gains on a global scale by shifting agricultural production to where it can best take place. It can also allow for a more efficient sourcing of the inputs to agricultural production. We need to remember that national boundaries were defined by a long historical game of musical chairs. While some sit on fertile lands, blessed with sunshine and fresh water, others are condemned to arid and inhospitable terrains. Trade imposed itself because differences across countries in terms of these natural endowments or in the productivity of labour cause differences in the relative efficiency of production (otherwise known as comparative advantage).

But there are other reasons for trade, too, such as economies of scale (which Nobel laureate Paul Krugman has told us all about). The efficiency gains brought about by international trade are also vital in light of the environmental challenges that we face. If a country such as Egypt were to aim for self-sufficiency in agriculture, it would soon need more than one River Nile. International trade in food is water saving. And, with the impending climate crisis, international trade in food will gain in importance as we come to the aid of drought-stricken countries.

Just like shirts, shoes and tyres?

Yet, in the WTO, members disagree on whether agriculture is just another good like shirts, shoes or tyres and should fall under the same trade regime. In other words, they disagree on whether the agricultural sector ought to be exposed to the same level of competition as other economic sectors. Efficient agricultural exporting countries, such as Brazil, believe that it should be, but others believe the opposite. The latter argue that labour-intensive subsistence agriculture, or production for local consumption, cannot compete in open markets against produce from highly capital-intensive agricultural systems. Agriculture is a sensitive political issue in many countries, both developing and developed.

As EU Trade Commissioner, I supported an overhaul of the European Union's significantly trade-distorting Common Agricultural Policy (CAP). Together with the then EU Agriculture Commissioner Franz Fischler, I pushed for the CAP reforms of 2004, which weakened the link between subsidies and production, arguably the policy's most trade-distorting element. It was clear that European farming needed support, but it was also clear that the support had to be much less distortive of trade. This was heresy for a Frenchman and it earned me the lasting enmity of the then French President Jacques Chirac, a former French farm minister. It is safe to say that we do not exchange Christmas cards.

Agriculture has long enjoyed special treatment at the WTO. It made its entry into the rulebook about fifty years after industrial goods and managed to do so on a different footing. For example, export subsidies, which are completely prohibited for industrial goods, are only to be phased out for agriculture in the Doha Round. Moreover, whereas trade-distorting subsidies for industrial goods are legally actionable in the WTO, many trade-distorting agricultural subsidies are permitted. The world's trade-weighted average industrial goods tariff is about 8 per cent, while in agriculture it is 25 per cent. And let's not forget tariff peaks, which in agriculture still rise up to 1,000 per cent.

As we have noted, the food crises triggered export restrictions. These restrictions had a domino, market-closing effect in 2008, with one restriction bringing about another as the world started to anticipate a global food shortage. The food importers reacted by asking for the restrictions to be lifted immediately. The surprising thing about this situation was that countries sitting on opposite sides of the export fence all expressed concerns about the same thing – namely, hunger. Some food-importing countries – China and South Korea are two examples – have responded by looking around for agricultural land to buy abroad – dubbed 'land grabs' by some.

As the multiple food crises were unfolding, we heard the United Nations Rapporteur on the Right to Food deliver the stark conclusion that we need 'to limit excessive reliance on international trade in the pursuit of food security'. I contested Olivier De Schutter's conclusion in a public debate with him in Geneva in 2009, and I still contest it today. Various farmers groups have also called for 'food sovereignty', by which they mean greater self-sufficiency. In his 2011 report 'The World Trade Organization and the Post-Global Food Crisis Agenda: Putting Food Security First in the International Food System', Professor De Schutter argues that food trade is not helping the poorest countries.

'The food bills of the least developed countries (LDCs) increased five- or six-fold between 1992 and 2008. Imports now account for around 25 per cent of their current food consumption. These countries are caught in a vicious cycle. The more they are told to rely on trade, the less they invest in domestic agriculture. And the less they support their own farmers, the more they have to rely on trade ... Unfortunately, the open markets demanded by Mr Lamy do not function as perfectly as he would like to think. Food moves where purchasing power is highest, not where needs are most urgent', he wrote in the report.

I agree with the rapporteur that food security is an essential policy objective for governments. Governments have a sovereign right to pursue policies to achieve food security within their international obligations. I also agree that the current state of global food security requires policies that encourage and strengthen investment in agriculture and ensure appropriate safety nets for urban and rural poor. But I fundamentally disagree with the assertion that countries need to limit reliance on international trade to achieve food security objectives. On the contrary, there is agreement among most UN-led experts that international trade is part of the package of solutions to achieve food security. The UN High-Level Task Force on the Global Food Security Crisis, in its 2010 Comprehensive Framework for Action, noted that 'more liberalized international markets would contribute to global food and nutrition security through increased trade volumes and access to diverse sources of food imports'.

With trade as part of a coherent macroeconomic and structural economic strategy, resources will tend towards an allocation based on comparative advantage, limiting inefficiencies. In response to an enhanced transmission of unbiased price signals, competitive producers adjust their production and investment decisions. This supply response helps to mitigate price pressure, contributing to improved availability of affordable food. Thus, trade can contribute to solutions to food security challenges. The WTO's Agreement on Agriculture leaves developing countries broad room to implement measures to achieve their national objectives, including food security. The Doha Round would further increase this flexibility, for example, when it comes to public stockholdings for food security purposes.

Policy tools, like public stockholding, safeguard measures to protect against import surges, or tariff rate quotas, under which duties vary according to whether the imported goods fall inside or outside volume limits set by the quotas, can be legitimate tools, under some circumstances. However, if used improperly, these actions can introduce distortions and undermine economic efficiency, exacerbating the negative impact on poor consumers of high food prices. In addition, given that about 60 per cent of developing countries' agricultural exports go to other developing countries, such moves increase the vulnerability of agricultural producers in exporting developing countries by reducing access to their main export markets.

Highly trade-distorting subsidies, the use of export subsidies, high levels of protection and unpredictable trade measures restricting imports or exports were – as we have noted – among the causes of food price spikes in 2008 and 2011. Policies that create distortions in the global market threaten rather than improve global food security. In agriculture, WTO rules distinguish between practices that are trade distorting and those with limited trade impacts – encouraging countries to move towards less trade-distorting practices.

'Starve-thy-neighbour'

Food security concerns require improved international governance. However, I am not convinced of the need to create new processes to discuss and evaluate food security and trade, as Professor De Schutter recommends. Many international, regional and national organizations already provide in-depth analysis of trade and food security. Clearly, international trade was not the source of the food crises. If anything, international trade has reduced the price of food over the years through greater competition and enhanced consumer purchasing power. International trade has also brought about undisputable efficiency gains in agricultural production.

But we must also understand the size of agricultural trade to put matters in context. International trade in agriculture is less than 10 per cent of world trade. Furthermore, whereas 50 per cent of the world's production of industrial goods enters international trade, only 25 per cent of the world's agricultural production is traded globally. In the case of rice, this figure drops to 5–7 per cent, making for a particularly thin international rice market. In addition, of the world's 25 per cent of food production that enters international trade, the vast majority (two-thirds) is processed food, and not rice, wheat or soybeans as some would like to claim. To suggest that less trade, and greater self-sufficiency, are the solutions to food security would be to argue that trade was itself to blame for the crisis, a proposition that would be difficult to sustain in light of the figures I have cited.

The world's thin rice markets are a case in point. Some have called the 2008 food crisis the 'rice price crisis'. It is because there is so little international trade in rice that prices reacted so dramatically to export restrictions. The limited international trade in rice made prices more, and not less, volatile. Deeper international commodity markets are less prone to such crises. I recall a meeting with members of the Yemeni government a few years back in which they complained of the 'starve-thy-neighbour' policies that followed the global food crisis of 2008. Yemen was being starved of its staple rice supply because of the numerous export restrictions imposed by others. Do we answer Yemen by recommending self-sufficiency? By recommending the same experiment that Saudi Arabia went through in growing its own wheat, and which it subsequently called off because of its heavy toll on water? Or do we answer Yemen by strengthening global interdependence and enhancing the reliability of international trade?

But we must ask ourselves why there is such widespread resentment to trade opening if such opening is indeed vital to global food security. To me the answer is clear. It is because we have yet to build robust safety nets for the world's poor. Each and every government must turn its attention to this issue – urgently, in my view. In the absence of such safety nets, there will always be resentment at a time of crisis to a country's food supply going abroad.

The Doha Round can bring about much-needed reform to agricultural trade policy. In fact, it is the developing world that placed the agricultural negotiations at the heart of the Doha Round, calling them the 'engine' of that trade round. The developing countries are seeking to redress what they see as a historical injustice in world trade rules; rules that allow the rich to continue to heavily subsidize their agriculture. The key instruction to agriculture negotiators is to achieve substantial improvements in the area of market access (i.e. tariff reduction) and substantial reductions in trade-distorting subsidies, together with the eventual elimination of all forms of export subsidies. And while countries have made substantial progress towards these goals, the last mile has yet to be completed.

But international trade, and indeed improvements to international trade rules through the Doha Round, would be only one component of better global agricultural policy. Agricultural policy starts at home and not at the international level. However, the reform of global trade rules and a better functioning international transmission belt for food are vital components of an enhanced food security picture.

Clearly, we must continue to aim for a shared vision of what global integration can bring to agriculture. International trade is not part of the problem but part of the solution to global food crises. The Doha Round – when completed – will oil the wheels of international trade in commodities, giving the developing world its fair share of the market. It will improve the workings of what is no more, in the end, than a transmission belt between countries where there is demand and countries where there is supply. For food trade, the climate crisis makes a properly functioning transmission belt even more imperative. Droughts, and other natural catastrophes, should not continue to deprive parts of the globe of food.

6

Trade can contribute towards better health

Anyone who has travelled widely in sub-Saharan Africa can have been left in little doubt about the catastrophic impact of the HIV/AIDS pandemic. From Uganda to South Africa, thousands of people, including small children, still die every day from the disease. I was devastated to see the suffering caused by HIV/AIDS during a trip to Southern Africa in 2001. And yet, thanks to an unprecedented UN-led global effort, the situation is beginning to improve as more and better drugs become available worldwide and global prevention programmes become more effective. But for a long time economic development was hampered and in some parts of Africa sent into reverse as the virus cut down men and women of working age. In many developing countries, HIV piled a huge new burden on already struggling or inadequate health and social services.

Global public health is a complex and teasing challenge, involving effective use of the full set of policy tools, both national and international. Trade is one of them, and within it, access to essential medicines for all remains the goal. Achieving it requires action across a wide front, from encouraging needed innovation, both medical and technological, to improving systems of health delivery. As the global disease burden evolves, so does the requirement for new and suitable medicines and technologies.

The priority settings for front-line treatments – whether more emphasis, for example, should be put on primary care – is a crucial issue, as are patterns of production and dissemination of medicines. All these are areas in which the World Health Organization (WHO) would be expected to take the lead. Consideration also needs to be given to domestic policies and practices, the infrastructure in a country and its national health system in general, as well as the transparency and efficiency of country drug-procurement regimes, which can have a huge impact on local prices and therefore the affordability of medicines.

The WTO's core mission of opening trade intersects with health in many ways, none of which can be treated in an isolated manner. International trade can help improve the health of people indirectly through economic growth and a corresponding improvement in incomes. There is a clear statistical correlation between poverty and health. Poor people in developing countries are more vulnerable to life-threatening infectious disease; they suffer higher rates of infant and maternal mortality, and they die younger. Nevertheless, as incomes rise, non-communicable diseases such as heart disease and cancer pose increasing threats to health and well-being in developing as well as developed countries. Health is a constantly evolving challenge.

Trade also influences health in a direct way. Open markets can improve the supply, quality and efficiency of medical supplies and services. Even the richest countries are not fully self-sufficient when it comes to the medical goods and services they consume, so trade helps them fill the gaps. This is even more the case for poorer developing countries with little in the way of domestic capacity to manufacture medicines. Trade can promote competition between suppliers, and, where there is real competition, goods tend to be both cheaper and more readily available. It is thanks to the competition among generic manufacturers that the cost of HIV/AIDS treatments has tumbled from over US$ 10,000 per patient per year in 2000 to around US$ 150 today. By increasing the range of suppliers, trade can improve the security of supply.

Trade policies, whether they are tariff levels, quotas or other regulations, also heavily influence affordability and availability of medicines. Tariffs make imported goods, including medicines, more expensive for consumers. This has led some to label tariffs, taxes and other charges on pharmaceuticals and other health-related products as a 'tax on health'. Some countries levy import duties on health supplies to protect local companies and ensure a degree of independence from international producers. Tariffs can also raise revenue for governments, although research shows that the amounts are not significant.

But because they come at the start of a local supply chain, tariffs can have a multiplier effect on the final price of medicines, which can take them beyond the financial reach of the poorer sections of society. Care must be taken that it is not only the better off in poor countries that benefit from the improved health services that more open markets can provide. Fortunately, the trend is towards the reduction or even elimination of tariffs. In developed countries, tariffs on medicines are already non-existent or very low. As for developing countries, average tariffs have also been falling over the past decade or so. Many developed countries, as well as several developing countries, participate in the WTO's pharmaceutical tariff initiative under which they agreed to remove tariffs on all finished pharmaceutical products and on certain active ingredients and manufacturing inputs.

Government procurement systems can also have a significant impact on access to medicines. Indeed, in many countries, government procurement programmes are responsible for the bulk of medical goods and services imported. These programmes aim to obtain medicines and other medical products of good quality, at the right time, in the right amounts and at the right price. But too often they achieve none of these goals due to inefficiency or even corruption. According to the World Bank, the procurement of medicines is particularly prone to poor administration, poor quality and price inflation. The WTO's plurilateral Government Procurement Agreement (GPA) provides an international framework of rules to promote transparency, fair competition and improved value for the public purse, which is increasingly important in these straightened fiscal times. In the health sector, this agreement has the potential to contribute substantially to improvement in the accessibility and affordability of medicines.

But merely ensuring access to the stock of existing, proven medicines is insufficient. As the son of pharmacists, having spent hours at the pharmacy that my parents owned in a suburb of Paris, I know that the current stock of medicines needs constant expansion to keep pace with the evolving disease burden. Simply to leverage access to an existing stock of drugs without encouraging the development of new medicines and new medical technologies would lead to diminishing returns. Effective access to essential medicines needs innovation, and innovation must be followed by access. This inexorable link has raised difficult questions about intellectual property (IP) rights and how they relate to the issue of universal access to affordable medicines.

All changed

The importance of public health is recognized in all WTO agreements, starting as far back as 1947 with the General Agreement on Tariffs and Trade (GATT), where the right of members to give priority to health policies was first spelled out. The Agreement on Sanitary and Phytosanitary (SPS) Measures, for example, says that governments can take any trade-related measure, including import bans, necessary to protect human life or health. These measures have to be justified by scientific evidence and they must be as least trade restricting as possible, but there is no doubt about the priority given to health over trade.

Nevertheless, health was rarely a subject for debate among trade ministers, traditionally more absorbed by issues such as industrial tariffs and farm subsidies. This all changed at the Doha ministerial meeting in 2001. There, trade ministers, including myself as EU Trade Commissioner, decided to respond to concerns that WTO rules on protecting IP might be hindering access to needed medicines in poorer countries and therefore harming the ability of these countries to respond to health emergencies such as HIV/AIDS.

The Uruguay Round introduced the protection of IP rights into the international trading system with the adoption of the Agreement on Trade-Related Aspects of Intellectual

Property Rights (TRIPS). But the issue of public health and its interplay with IP rules, which can affect trade in medicines, had not been properly addressed at the WTO. In their 'Doha Declaration on the TRIPS Agreement and Public Health', ministers made clear that the TRIPS Agreement did not and should not prevent members from taking measures to protect public health.

Intellectual property covers a host of questions, from copyright and related rights to trademarks, industrial designs and patents. Essentially IP rights are intended to ensure that creators have the right to be paid for the use of their inventions, designs or ideas. The TRIPS Agreement for the first time laid down basic levels of protection that countries had to give to the IP of their fellow WTO members. But some developing countries, and many non-governmental organizations (NGOs), viewed the agreement as an impediment to efforts to combat public health emergencies. They felt that the TRIPS Agreement restricted drug availability, essentially because they saw it limiting access to generic drugs.

One definition of 'generic' is that it is a product without a trademark. When it comes to medicines, 'paracetamol' would be an example. The TRIPS Agreement has nothing to say about trade in such medicines. But generics can also be 'copies' of patented drugs or medicines whose patents have expired, and it is here that IP rules can affect availability and where the argument between those who backed the TRIPS Agreement and those who opposed it centred and still centres.

In the developed world, pharmaceutical industries view the TRIPS Agreement as being essential to encouraging innovation by ensuring adequate international compensation to the pharmaceutical sector for its research, development and creativity. In the absence of such compensation, the industry insists, it could not recoup the high costs of developing new life-saving drugs. The issue of IP is one of the most emotive and, consequently, frequently debated issues when it comes to trade and public health. As recognized by the Doha Declaration and reiterated in several WHO resolutions, we are talking here about a delicate balancing act between guaranteeing the protection of IP rights as an important incentive for the development of new medicines on the one hand, and addressing concerns about the potential impact on prices for such medicines on the other hand.

The Doha Declaration recognized that the IP system is not an isolated specialist domain, nor yet a monolithic barrier to public health. Instead, ministers saw IP as an element in the complex set of policy tools required to solve global problems. The logic of the Doha Declaration remains compelling today. The Doha Declaration helped catalyse the growing understanding that access to medicines requires the right mix of health policies, IP rules and trade policy settings, and involves the judicious and informed use of a range of measures, including competition policy, drug procurement strategies, attention to tariffs and other trade-related drivers of cost, and choices within the IP system. In other words, it requires policy coherence. Coherence, as in so many other aspects of trade-related policy, is key to finding sustainable solutions.

In practical terms, the declaration allowed WTO member governments to tackle a specific problem with the Agreement as it then stood: it called on the WTO to find a way to allow all countries to make effective use of compulsory licences to manufacture generic medicines. Compulsory licensing is when a government authorizes a company to make a medicine – or any other product – without the permission of the patent owner. The TRIPS Agreement allowed compulsory licences for the production of generic medicines, provided such licences would be used 'predominantly' for the supply of the domestic market of the member authorizing such use.

Some argued that this provision could limit exports to countries that did not have the manufacturing capacity to make medicines for themselves. This was important because the poorest countries, with no or insufficient manufacturing capacity of their own, were the ones most vulnerable to HIV/AIDS and other major health threats. In 2003, the WTO announced a waiver on the 'limitation to export' restriction and finally agreed to convert this into a fully fledged amendment to the TRIPS Agreement in 2005. The decision was taken even though it ruffled feathers among those who felt it was not really the WTO's role to promote access to medicines. But for the developing world, the issue of compulsory licences was an important test as to whether the WTO could meet their developmental needs.

Prices and access

So far only Canada has made use of the TRIPS waiver with two shipments to Rwanda in 2008 and 2009 of the HIV antiretroviral (ARV) drug – Apo-TriAvir. In part, this restricted use of the WTO waiver flows from the limited patent coverage of needed medicines in key exporting countries. Where a patent is not recognized, waivers are not needed. Pharmaceutical companies in India, which did not recognize patents on medicines until 2005, produce more than 80 per cent of donor-funded ARVs supplied to developing countries. So we may see increased use of the TRIPS mechanism as future procurement efforts turn towards a new generation of medicines. Developed countries have dominated trade in health-related products, but China and India have emerged as leading global exporters, and some other developing countries have also shown strong export growth. But the very existence of the waiver, together with the changing climate among the health community and drug companies, can help drug procurement programmes to bargain down prices – just as the prospect of compulsory licensing can be used in general to exert leverage in negotiations on voluntary access to technologies.

Voluntary licensing, where patent owners agree to the copying of their product, often emerges as an operationally more effective tool in many cases. Most pharmaceutical companies that hold patents for their HIV/AIDS medicines have signed voluntary licence agreements with various generic producers, a trend that increased after the adoption of the waiver.

In any case, the objective was never to issue lots of compulsory licences. The objective was and remains cheaper medicines for the poor. The system, therefore, has to be judged in terms of prices and access. A simple headcount of notifications under the waiver, known as the 'paragraph 6 mechanism' after the relevant paragraph in the Doha

Declaration, is a poor indicator of improvements in public health. The paragraph 6 system is one additional element of flexibility within the TRIPS Agreement, alongside a number of other health policy safeguards; and the TRIPS Agreement itself in turn forms just one element of wider national and international action to ensure enhanced access to medicines.

Indeed, the TRIPS Agreement explicitly recognizes the need to create economies of scale for procurement initiatives in regions with a significant proportion of LDCs. We also need to assess the operation of this system against a stronger empirical base – put simply: where are relevant medical patents in force, and where are they not? These deceptively simple questions can be hard to answer with confidence.

The UN's World Intellectual Property Organization (WIPO) has made great strides to improve access to, and intelligent use of, patent information, and to facilitate international co-operation to establish the patent status of key medicines in developing countries. Here again, multilateral co-operation is essential to ensure that this mechanism operates effectively, along with the full range of policy tools, within and beyond the field of IP, to step up the flow of essential medicines to those who most need them.

A more general concern is often expressed about so-called TRIPS 'plus' provisions in preferential trade agreements (PTAs), either bilateral agreements or regional ones. Certain of the provisions concerned – such as provisions reinforcing the protection of undisclosed test data submitted in support of applications for marketing approval of pharmaceutical products – may potentially have a bearing on access to medicines, as well as on the generic industry. At the same time, developed country members participating in such PTAs have recently confirmed their commitment to 'access to medicines for all', stating that such provisions are not meant to affect the ability of the parties to take measures to protect public health.

The WTO's role in all this remains limited: the TRIPS Agreement tells us that members are free to adopt higher standards of protection. Therefore, the WTO can at best monitor the content of such PTAs and offer a platform for discussion, as it does, for example, in the trade policy reviews of members. Any more ambitious initiative has to come from the membership, the WTO being a member-driven organization. But the main responsibility lies within national governments, including how IP is handled in PTAs. If governments accept tougher standards for IP protection than required in the TRIPS Agreement, then governments are accountable to their critics, not to the WTO.

The Doha Declaration also led the WTO to step up the technical assistance it gives to developing countries on understanding various flexibilities granted under the TRIPS Agreement, including compulsory licensing and parallel importing. Parallel importing is when a product made legally (i.e. not pirated) abroad is imported without the permission of the IP right-holder. Some countries allow parallel imports, but others do not.

More importantly, the Doha Declaration saw a shift in focus from a more passive view of the 'compatibility' of trade, IP and health to a more dynamic and constructive search for 'coherence' between them. It allowed a more effective partnership to develop between the WHO, WIPO and the WTO. The WHO brings to the table a vast expertise in the areas of essential medicines, regulatory questions, pricing and other factors affecting access to medicines. WIPO is uniquely placed to help the WTO work towards a truly global view of information on the patent status of key medicines in developing countries, and to lend its expertise on patent law and its interplay with public policy.

The Doha Declaration helped shape the framework for multilateral co-operation in health, including the provision of technical and policy support mentioned above, the editing of joint publications and the organization of participant exchanges for training programmes. In 2007 WIPO's annual general assembly issued a specific instruction to the agency to intensify co-operation on IP-related issues with relevant international organizations, and in particular with the WHO and the WTO. Similarly, in 2008 the annual World Health Assembly requested the WHO Director-General 'to coordinate with other relevant international intergovernmental organizations', including WIPO and the WTO.

Policy coherence

One of the most significant manifestations of this co-operation was a combined study published in early 2013 by the WTO, the WHO and WIPO entitled 'Promoting Access to Medical Technologies and Innovation'. As the foreword said, the collaboration reflected:

> a practical necessity for the WHO, WIPO and WTO
> secretariats to coordinate and cooperate ever more closely

on issues such as patterns of innovation and access,
legal and policy factors affecting the production and
dissemination of medical technologies, and the interplay
between public health, international trade rules and the
intellectual property (IP) system.

For example, effective use of TRIPS flexibilities for public
health requires improved access to patent information, a core
WIPO function, and is guided by detailed information on
disease burdens, medicine prices and patterns of access, data
that is a particular focus of the WHO. The study is one of the
many bridges the WTO constructed with other international
organizations during my tenure.

So, while fundamentally important for the WTO and
for the application of the TRIPS Agreement, the Doha Declaration helped to change the policy environment and shape
the framework for multilateral co-operation on IP and public
health. The way innovation and invention lead to economic
and social benefits also changed. I doubt the Medicines
Patent Pool would have been feasible before. The Pool is a
United Nations-backed, Geneva-based organization that aims
to lower the prices of HIV medicines and facilitate the development of better-adapted HIV medicines in developing
countries by entering into voluntary licensing agreements
with manufacturers. It was founded in 2010 at the request
of the international community through the WHO-based
financing mechanism UNITAID. Created in 2006, UNITAID
is an international drug purchase facility. The objective of
this facility is to scale up access to prevention and treatment
products for HIV/AIDS, TB and malaria in developing
countries.

The WTO has served as an active and constructive partner on public health within the multilateral system. The effective use of the IP system and of TRIPS flexibilities is important, but does not stand alone: IP law and policy must be harnessed with drug procurement policies, pro-competition safeguards and regulation of drugs for safety and quality. Again, no one international agency has a monopoly on these diverse areas of expertise, and the challenge of ensuring practical access to medicines requires a comprehensive, multidisciplinary effort.

Infectious diseases certainly do not respect borders; they prey upon our common physiology, blind to political boundaries, as the rapid spread of potentially dangerous new flu viruses such as bird flu has shown in recent years. Health represents the most compelling case for international co-operation. Interdependence is not a mere policy option; it is quite literally a matter of life and death.

7

Trade and labour: separated at birth, but still connected

The Centre William Rappard, home of the WTO, on the shores of Lake Léman in Geneva, was inaugurated in 1926 to house the International Labour Organization (ILO), which subsequently moved to another location in 1975. The building hosts a number of very interesting works of art celebrating labour, donated to the ILO over the years by trade unions and employee associations. Many of these works were covered up when the building became home to the WTO, as if to erase all links between trade and employment. When the renovation of the building began in 2006, many of these works of art were unveiled and are now on display to visitors. This was not simply an artistic gesture, but a reminder that trade and jobs cannot be separated.

The current crisis has revived the debate on the implications of trade policies for employment. The ILO tells us that there are 28 million more people unemployed around the world today than in 2007, and unemployment has risen to record levels in the industrialized world. Developing countries have also been affected. While the number of people without a job rose by 4.2 million in 2012, only a quarter of those concerned live in developed countries; the rest are in other regions, in particular East Asia, South Asia and sub-Saharan Africa.

Globalization and trade opening are sometimes perceived – particularly in developed countries, but increasingly also in the developing world – as having a negative impact on employment. Today's debate on trade and employment is nothing new. As a matter of fact, it was concern over mass unemployment in the 1930s – resulting from devastating protectionist policies – that prompted policy makers in the post-World War Two period to draw up an entirely new system of international economic governance. Its purpose was to better articulate and manage the links between full employment, social progress, development, the international monetary system and trade opening.

The future system was to rest on three pillars. Two of the global pillars were the International Monetary Fund (IMF) and the World Bank, both of which emerged from the Bretton Woods Conference of 1944. The third was to be the International Trade Organization (ITO), which was formally accepted by fifty-three countries in 1948 with the approval of the Havana Charter, named after the Cuban capital where final negotiations were held. Preparatory work on the Charter had begun in 1946 following a resolution of the Economic and Social Council of the United Nations that called for 'an international conference on trade and employment for the purpose of promoting the expansion of the production, exchange and consumption of goods'. Note the conjunction of the words 'trade' and 'employment'.

Full employment was enshrined as a principal goal in the opening article of the Charter and the second of its nine chapters was devoted to employment and economic activity. Beyond the general issue of employment, the chapter contained specific provisions on fair labour standards. Its Article 7 declared that members 'recognize that unfair labour conditions, particularly in production for export, create difficulties in international trade, and, accordingly, each member shall take whatever action may be appropriate and feasible to eliminate such conditions within its territory'. Commercial policy, including tariffs, preferences, internal taxation and regulation, was covered in chapter 4 of the Charter.

While discussions on the ITO had proceeded, a smaller group of developed and developing countries had held parallel talks on tariff cuts. These negotiations concluded successfully in 1947 with the signing of the General Agreement on Tariffs and Trade (GATT). The idea was that the GATT formed the chapter on trade in the forthcoming Charter of the ITO. But although the Charter was delivered, the ITO arrived stillborn. In the United States, big business, suspicious of the social and labour clauses in the ITO agreement, lobbied hard against it, and in 1950 President Harry Truman announced that he would no longer seek Senate support for the Charter. That was the end of the ITO, and its demise left the ersatz GATT as the only international trade body. The GATT lasted until it was replaced by the WTO in 1994.

In many ways, the GATT can be seen as an ITO minus the elements of economic policy coherence. Even though the preambles to the GATT and the Marrakesh Agreement establishing the WTO include references to 'ensuring full employment', neither treaty makes the link between opening trade and fair labour standards, which was an integral part of the ITO accords.

The term labour standards embraces many issues, ranging from child and forced labour, the right to organize trade unions and to strike, to questions such as minimum wages, health and safety conditions and working hours. True, virtually all WTO governments are members of the International Labour Organization (ILO) and as such have committed to a set of internationally recognized 'core' labour standards – freedom of association, no forced labour, no child labour and no discrimination at work (including gender discrimination). But the WTO itself is not a standard-setting organization, neither for labour issues nor for matters related to the safety of food or industrial products.

Nevertheless, a number of attempts were made in the early years of the WTO to link trade opening and labour standards. At the 1996 Singapore Ministerial Conference, the first following the launch of the WTO, members declared that the ILO was the competent body to negotiate labour standards, not the WTO. They noted, however, that further trade opening could contribute to the promotion of these standards. They rejected the use of labour standards for protectionist purposes and agreed that the comparative advantage of certain countries, particularly low-wage developing countries, must in no way be put into question.

There was another attempt to raise the issue at the Seattle ministerial in 1999, and two years later a paragraph reaffirming the declaration made at the Singapore Ministerial Conference regarding core labour standards was included in the Doha Ministerial Declaration.

Labour standards and trade is a complex issue. Advocates of the theory of 'social dumping', mainly in developed countries, argue that high labour standards, particularly when it comes to minimum wages and health and safety conditions, come at a cost. This cost, they argue, affects their ability to compete in global markets, so standards should be harmonized internationally. Others, mainly developing countries, view this as an attempt at 'social protectionism'. These countries assert that imposing harmonization from outside would undermine their comparative advantage when it comes to wage costs and hinder economic development.

The fact that WTO members have refused to get involved in the setting and monitoring of labour standards does not mean that the question of employment has not been an important part of the debate on trade opening. Jobs, their creation or loss, are at the centre of discussion within countries when it comes to weighing up the perceived benefits or otherwise of open markets. In developed countries, some see globalization, and growing imports in particular, as one of the prime causes of a noticeable decline in the number of jobs available in their manufacturing industries.

The trade versus jobs fallacy

As we have seen in earlier chapters, trade opening creates greater efficiencies, encourages innovation and generates wealth. But this does not mean that trade opening is good for every person, every country, every time – as Abraham Lincoln might have said. There is little question that greater competition puts companies and indeed entire sectors of an economy under pressure. Economists agree that trade is responsible for some job losses in the United States and other developed countries in recent years. Over the last sixty years, the share of people employed in the manufacturing industry in

99

the United States has fallen from 33 per cent of civilian non-agricultural employment to less than 10 per cent. Britain, France and even Germany have also seen industrial employment drop sharply just as China has emerged as the 'factory of the world'. Some – but by no means all – of the wage stagnation that has beset workers in developed countries is likewise often blamed on competition from lower-wage country exporters.

In fact, trade plays only a small part in overall job destruction. Harvard professor Bob Lawrence, an expert in international trade, has estimated that only a little over one in ten manufacturing jobs lost in the decade to 2008 in the United States was lost due to international trade, with losses due in large part to a sharp rise in productivity. Other studies put the figure somewhere between 4 and 15 per cent. The surge in productivity growth has been brought about by technological innovation, which means that fewer workers are needed to produce more.

The economic rise of China and India and other emerging countries has meant the integration of tens, if not hundreds, of millions of workers into the global economy in the past two decades. What is astonishing is that this integration occurred at the same time unemployment rates in OECD and eurozone countries were declining. Between 1998 and 2008, the average unemployment rate in the euro area fell from 9.9 per cent to 7.4 per cent – obviously it has jumped back up as a result of the crisis – while the corresponding reduction among OECD countries was from 6.6 per cent to 5.9 per cent.

If international trade is a zero-sum game, as some would have us believe, the economic rise of these countries should have thrown millions of workers in the developed world out of work. But international trade is not a zero-sum game. The problem with the argument that trade destroys jobs is that it sees only the threat posed by imports to jobs, but does not take into consideration how jobs may be created in the export sector as a consequence of trade opening. It also fails to take into account that trade opening can increase the rate of economic growth – by increasing the rate of capital accumulation and by speeding up technological progress through innovation or knowledge creation – and therefore improve the ability of an economy to create new jobs.

Trade as creator not destroyer

Exports can increase the levels and growth rates of income or output as they often have a high value-added component. This is especially true in developed countries, where firms specialize in the high value-added segment of the global supply chain. Importantly, the value-added component of exports is likely to have a positive effect on domestic demand due to backward linkages with several sectors in the economy. In fact, evidence suggests that the domestic content of value added by exports, something we discussed in Chapter 2, is higher as countries develop. For example, in 2008, 80 per cent of the value of the goods exported by the United States had a domestic content, while this share was only 42 per cent for Malaysia.

Of course, one must remember that not all the jobs created in export-oriented sectors will go to previously unemployed workers. Some will go to previously employed workers who are transferring to the export sector because of better opportunities. Even so, this reallocation is economically valuable. It means that workers are moving from sectors where their marginal productivity is lower to those where it is higher. This results in productivity gains to the economy and hence increased output and employment. But given the current high rates of unemployment, particularly in parts of Europe, it is likely that many of those getting these jobs in the export sector will be from the ranks of the unemployed.

It must also be acknowledged that with import competition and outsourcing, trade may lead to job losses in certain sectors of the economy. This is where domestic programmes to train workers and help them develop new skills, and to foster greater mobility in labour markets, can enable those displaced to find jobs in the more efficient, expanding sectors of the economy. In a world where markets are characterized by rapid technological changes and where value creation matters more than ever, being able to develop and mobilize new skills that can match ever-changing market conditions becomes paramount, both for workers and for companies. This is also where social safety nets can help workers to bear the burden of transition in the short run. Nordic countries such as Sweden and Finland offer examples of economies that have combined significant levels of labour market flexibility with strong social safety nets. But the key point is that trade can have a positive impact on incomes or output and job creation during the economic downturn. But for this to happen, international markets must remain open and countries must continue to trade on the basis of comparative advantage.

When it comes to poorer countries, a country that opens up trade and improves its business environment may become more attractive to foreign investors with more foreign capital flowing to its shores. Since technology is often embodied in goods, trade can be a very effective means of diffusing technological know-how. In developing countries, trade can increase productivity through 'learning-by-exporting', whereby participation in world production chains enables producers to lower costs or move up the value-added chain over time. Trade can increase income or output levels through efficiency gains from specialization based on comparative advantage, greater competition, access to a larger variety of intermediate inputs, economies of scale and an intra-industry reallocation of resources.

Trade also allows external demand to provide a buffer for economies facing low domestic demand during periods of recovery from a crisis, such as the one that began in 2008. This is especially important in several developed economies, where domestic demand was subdued for a while as domestic savings were reconstituted and the financial system recovered. Trade openness vis-à-vis a diverse set of countries is important for mediating the effect of a shock.

The message is particularly pertinent to Europe. In my own country, France, the prolonged economic crisis resurrected the old debate on whether French industry and agriculture would benefit from more protectionism. Opinion polls suggested that a majority of voters thought they would. But protectionism, as I have argued throughout this book, offers a weak defence against an economic crisis. The best protection for any economy is attack, attack on the export front. Germany's economic performance in the early years of this century – before the economic crisis began in 2008 – offers a good example of how export strength and competitiveness can help drive an economy when domestic demand is sluggish.

Our experience from past recessions suggests that employment growth will be slow in the aftermath of a crisis even though output expansion may have resumed. During the 'dotcom' crisis, for example, the US economy stopped contracting in November 2001 and began growing again in terms of output. But the unemployment rate continued to climb until June 2003, nineteen months later. One reason commonly advanced to explain such 'jobless recoveries' is the uncertainty faced by employers about whether the economic expansion they are witnessing is sustainable. Only if they are convinced that demand growth is durable will they be willing to commit to new hiring. This is why the conclusion of the Doha Round could contribute to reducing uncertainty relating to protectionism, the spectre of which may hinder new hiring, especially in the export sector, since it is the most vulnerable to trade restrictions.

I have argued that trade generates employment overall. But what of the charge that growing trade drives governments in rich countries to permit lower social or labour standards? This is the 'race to the bottom' argument, and it is also a fallacy. The great problem with this argument is that there is very little empirical basis for it. It is difficult to find examples where countries have lowered social or labour standards in response to trade competition. French historian and political scientist Emmanuel Todd uses one variant of this argument when he claims that open trade between developing countries, such as China, and industrial countries is the reason for the economic crisis. In his view, the competition coming from low-wage countries has put pressure on wages in industrial countries and caused a deficiency in aggregate demand.

I would argue that differences in wages largely reflect differences in labour productivity. There is a fairly close correlation between wages and productivity across countries, with some estimates going so far as to suggest that 90 per cent of wage differences between countries can be explained by productivity differences. While wages in many developing countries may be low, labour productivity in these countries is also a fraction of Western levels, and we have also seen wages in many developing countries, including China, significantly increase in recent years.

Finally, some also argue that trade has been responsible for the observed widening of the gap in the wages of skilled and unskilled workers in industrial countries. However, much of this gap can be explained by skill-biased technological change rather than by trade. Skill-biased technological change refers to improvements in technology, such as the information technology revolution, which increased demand for skilled workers relative to unskilled workers. In the United States, this technological change combined with the slowdown in the relative supply of college-equivalent workers led to the expansion of wage differentials between skilled and unskilled workers. Some – but only some – of the wage stagnation that has beset American workers can also be blamed on competition from lower-wage country exporters.

Not every country, every person, every time

Trade can create jobs, but this has not automatically translated into better quality employment, particularly in poorer developing countries. Trade opening needs proper domestic policies to create good jobs, or what the ILO calls 'decent' work. A joint study by the ILO and the WTO in 2009 found that high levels of informal employment in the developing world cut the benefits to countries from trade opening by creating poverty traps.

The study, a product of the collaborative research programme of the ILO International Institute for Labour Studies and the WTO Secretariat, focused on the link between globalization and informal employment. It found that informal employment was widespread in many developing countries, leaving thousands of workers with almost no job security, low incomes and no social protection. Levels of informality varied substantially across countries, ranging from as low as 30 per cent in some Latin American countries to more than 80 per cent in certain sub-Saharan African and South Asian countries.

Informal employment involves private, unregistered enterprises that are not subject to national law or regulation, offer no social protection and involve self-employed individuals, or members of the same household. The study showed that more open economies tend to have a lower incidence of informal employment. The short-term effects of trade reforms may in the first instance be associated with higher informal employment. But longer-term effects point in the direction of a strengthening of formal sector employment, provided that trade reforms are more employment friendly and the right domestic policies are in place.

The report said that making it easier for firms and workers to operate in the formal sector helps a country to benefit fully from trade openness, improves living standards and gives workers access to decent working conditions. Social protection is also crucial for supporting transitions to more open trading systems and realizing the gains from open trade. So great attention should be devoted to social protection policies as well as to the design of trade reforms.

Policies that support adjustment cost money and cannot always be easily or extensively developed by poorer countries. This may in turn influence the pace at which governments choose to open up to trade. The fact that trade opening may lead to an initial increase in informal employment does not, in my opinion, invalidate the case for trade opening. The evidence of the benefits from trade opening is overwhelming, but the reality of adjustment costs does caution against an easy assumption that simply opening to trade is a sufficient condition for securing development and greater prosperity for all.

Trade and labour policy coherence

We began this chapter with the formal breaking of the link between trade, job creation and labour standards at the birth of the global institutions set up after World War Two to guide economic and social policy making. But as the joint ILO-WTO study demonstrates, issues relating to employment and labour standards continue to generate trade concerns that the WTO cannot ignore. For this reason, the ILO and the WTO have sought to deepen their co-operation in recent years.

The 2009 study is one example of this evolving relationship. Trade and labour policies overlap and interact; the greater the policy coherence between the two organizations, the more likely it is that trade can bring benefits through both greater economic growth and more 'decent' jobs. That was the main conclusion of a joint research project into trade and employment carried out by the ILO and the WTO in 2007. The importance of this coherence was reaffirmed in the ILO's 2008 'Declaration on Social Justice for a Fair Globalization', which recognized the potential benefits of globalization, but also called for renewed efforts to implement decent work policies. 'The violation of fundamental principles and rights at work cannot be invoked or otherwise used as a legitimate comparative advantage and . . . labour standards should not be used for protectionist trade purposes', it stated.

But here we should note that it is not enough to have standards, whether they are labour standards, building standards or any other kind of rules and regulations designed for the safety of working people, if they are not applied rigorously. The collapse of a factory building outside Dhaka, the capital of Bangladesh, in April 2013, in which over 1,000 people died, is a chilling case in point. There are still many countries where workers' rights, even where they exist on paper, are not honoured in practice. Sometimes these workers form parts of global supply chains, whose goods end up in the shops of developed and richer developing countries. In such instances, there is also a moral obligation on the part of international companies to ensure that all production along the chain meets acceptable labour and safety standards.

As we have seen, the way to introducing labour standards into WTO agreements seems barred, at least for the present. At the international level, social questions remain the domain of ILO conventions and regulations. But beyond the co-operation represented by research projects and joint studies, is there room for more concrete connections or bridges between the ILO's decent work programme and the WTO?

Perhaps one route could be for the ILO to get more directly involved in evaluating the employment effects of trade policies, as suggested in its 2008 declaration. As a first step, the ILO could request observer status at the WTO. Observer status, which is granted for individual WTO bodies and committees, allows intergovernmental organizations to follow discussions on matters of direct interest to them. The Committee on Trade and Development attracts the highest number of observers, with nearly thirty international organizations formally accredited, while several others have access on an ad hoc basis. This could be the WTO body of most direct relevance to the ILO. Or a new Committee on Trade and Employment could be created. Whichever way, I believe that the oddity that the WTO has observer status in the ILO but that the reverse is not the case should be fixed. After all, WTO members are all ILO members and coherence on this matter is long overdue.

The ILO could also take a more direct approach to the monitoring of trade and labour standards. In cases where it believes there to be serious violations of its labour standards by a member country, it could recommend that sanctions be applied to encourage the erring member to mend its ways. Article 37 (2) of the ILO constitution envisages the creation of a tribunal for the resolution of disputes and questions arising from the interpretation of ILO regulations, although no such tribunal has yet been set up. Sanctions, of course, would be a very serious step, a sort of 'nuclear option', to be contemplated only as a final resort.

The interdependency between trade measures and domestic or international policies, including working conditions, is a recurrent theme that goes to the heart of the case for open trade. We understand much better today than in the past how economic development is influenced by the broader setting in which trade openness is fostered. Reaping the full benefits of trade requires that other conditions are present, including flexible labour markets, an adequate set of skills and strong social safety nets.

8

Trade and energy: the case for a greater WTO role

A decade ago only two of the world's top five oil-producing countries were members of the WTO. Today Iran is the only country in the top ten oil producers that does not belong to the trade body. Only two of the world's top ten gas producers are not WTO members; again Iran is one and the other is Algeria. But both Iran and Algeria want to join, as do all the other important energy-producing countries that remain outside the WTO, including Iraq, Libya and Sudan. The WTO already gathers under its roof countries responsible for the bulk of the world's energy output and could soon house all of them. Yet the WTO is not as involved as it could and perhaps should be in helping oversee the world's energy trade, which is an area where global governance could be improved.

Energy accounts for a significant part of world trade, but the WTO has relatively little to say about it. When the rules of the GATT were negotiated some sixty-five years ago, opening trade in energy was not a political priority. World energy demand was a fraction of what it is today and a barrel of crude oil went for US$ 20 at current prices, less than a fifth of the cost in early 2013. The world economy has changed dramatically since the 1940s and so have the energy challenges. The economic growth rates of many developing countries will inevitably push up global energy demand and make equitable access to supplies an ever more pressing issue. More energy production can lead to more pollution, so rising energy consumption will need to be reconciled with sustainable growth if we are to tackle the challenges presented by climate change. Massive private investments will be necessary to respond to the needs of research in green energy technologies, namely in renewable energy sources and energy efficiency, and investors will demand the reassurance of clear international rules and regulations.

But energy products have a number of special characteristics that make them different from products in sectors such as manufacturing and agriculture and less susceptible to a WTO-style trade regime. Markets play a part in the economics of energy supply and demand, but in a rather more complicated way than what a standard textbook would tell us about the workings of markets and the role of international trade. Let us briefly consider some of the reasons for this.

First, much of today's energy supply – particularly fossil fuels and natural gas – is geographically concentrated, fixed in terms of location and prominent in the production and trade of the countries that possess the resource. Thus, trade patterns on the supply side are largely predetermined and change only slowly in contrast to the shifting comparative advantage we associate with countries less dependent on or less well endowed with natural resources.

Compared to the geographical concentration that characterizes the supply side of energy markets, demand is very widely spread, because all countries need energy to run their economies. This relationship between supply and demand has important implications for the economic and political conditions under which trade takes place. A second feature of today's key energy products is that they are scarce and non-renewable. Combined with their fixed and concentrated location, this makes for less direct competition in production and the presence of significant economic rents.

Thirdly, natural resource sectors tend to display a high degree of price volatility. While no leading economic model explains the causes of such volatility, contributing factors include supply uncertainties, inelastic demand due to the lack, in the short run, of substitutes for traditional energy products, and the role of speculation and political uncertainty in some producing countries. This combination of circumstances means that trade does not enhance competition and adjust resource allocation in the standard 'Ricardian' manner that we think of in relation to trade in manufactured goods, agriculture and services.

The physical characteristics of energy goods – whether gas, oil or electricity – affect the way in which they are transported across borders and distributed to final consumers. The existence of natural monopolies and the role of state-owned enterprises also influence the way energy markets work. Sovereignty and strategic concerns figure much more prominently in the energy sector than in other areas of trade, creating greater reluctance to enter into new internationally binding agreements.

Notwithstanding these special characteristics, the WTO's basic rules are in principle applicable to all forms of trade, including trade in energy goods and services. And these rules can be enforced through the WTO dispute settlement mechanism. Having said this, WTO rules, which were not negotiated with the special characteristics of the energy sector in mind, may not address appropriately all the needs of energy trade. For example, back in the 1970s and 1980s, governments tried but failed under the GATT to tackle the issues of dual pricing for domestic and export markets and export restrictions on raw materials.

Moreover, WTO rules are based on a distinction between goods and services, but it is not always easy to categorize trade in the energy sector as belonging to one or the other. For example: when oil is refined, is it a service or a good that is being supplied? Some argue that oil refining is a service, but others consider that it amounts to the production of a good, because the refining process creates a new product. The question of whether electricity should be considered a good or a service has remained unsettled for the last sixty years.

It is not just a theoretical issue, but has practical and legal consequences when it comes to applying WTO rules. Why so? Because there are major differences between the WTO rules that deal with goods and the rules that deal with services, and the differences have major implications for the way in which this sector gets regulated. For example, the WTO's General Agreement on Trade in Services (GATS) only covers those services that members agree to subject to its disciplines, so not all energy services are necessarily included. In contrast, all trade in goods is subject to the disciplines of the General Agreement on Tariffs and Trade (GATT).

Energy appears on the WTO radar

In recent years, energy has begun to appear increasingly on the radar screen of WTO members, while at the same time the WTO has loomed ever larger on the radar screens of the energy business community. This reflects the significant changes that have taken place in energy markets, which some argue fortify the case for closer attention on the part of the WTO to the energy sector. Energy was not addressed in any comprehensive manner during the Uruguay Round, because liberalization of the sector was not yet on the political agenda. As a result, WTO members undertook limited commitments to open their markets to foreign operators in energy services, including services related to the exploitation of oil and gas fields, energy distribution and pipeline transportation of fuels. However, progressive unbundling of state-owned integrated utilities and technological developments have created room for private operators. This, in turn, has raised the profile of energy services in the WTO.

Over time a larger number of players have entered the field on the supply side. In no small part, this is the result of technological advances and the diversification of energy sources. Fossil fuels and natural gas increasingly compete with alternative energy sources, such as nuclear power and renewables, including biofuels, wind, water and solar power. The trend towards embracing renewable sources of energy will continue as concerns about global warming intensify. Climate change, and how we can secure international co-operation to combat it, has become a central preoccupation of the global policy community. This carries significant implications for energy markets as it may lead to an increasing use of renewable energy resources, thus decreasing the share of conventional energy. According to an OECD study, global greenhouse gas emissions could be 10 per cent lower in 2050 if emerging economies and developing countries removed their subsidies on fossil fuel consumption. The use of subsidies to produce and promote renewable energy is an issue that looms larger in the WTO, as we shall see below.

Furthermore, many countries, but particularly the United States, are expanding use of hydraulic fracturing, more commonly known as 'fracking', to generate oil and gas. Fracking, which remains controversial because of the environmental risks it can pose, is changing the face of global energy production. It has turned the United States into the world's largest producer of natural gas and along the way reduced its dependence on international oil supplies.

I am not suggesting that the structure of the energy market will change overnight, but rather that the panorama is changing and that this reinforces the case for examining how an institution like the WTO, its rules and its forums might contribute to an orderly and mutually beneficial framework for international co-operation in the energy field. The increased relevance of the WTO to energy also comes from the fact that – as we noted – major energy-exporting countries have joined the organization in recent years, including Oman, Saudi Arabia and Russia. The purpose and principles of the WTO are clearly applicable to energy trade. Non-discrimination, transparency, an explicit structure of rules that provides predictability and reduces arbitrariness in trade relations, greater openness over time, and a mechanism for settling disputes constitute the foundations of the WTO system and can benefit energy trade governance.

Many GATT rules are very relevant to trade in natural resources and energy, but this happens by default rather than design because the rules, as we have noted, were not drawn up with these sectors in mind. The reason is that the prime concern of the WTO is to open up export markets and to do this it focuses on limiting import restrictions and domestic market distortions, such as subsidies. But when it comes to energy trade, restrictions on imports are never going to be much of an issue, because consuming countries are more interested in facilitating access rather than limiting it. Practices prohibited under the GATT, but still prevalent in energy trade, include trade-distorting subsidies, certain anti-competitive practices by state trading enterprises, transit restrictions for transporting energy, energy export restrictions, or restrictions on the movement of energy service providers, like oil extracting and drilling companies. In recent years, members have brought a number of energy-related disputes to the WTO, citing rules on subsidies, local-content requirements or export restrictions, among others.

Many of the disputes have to do with renewable energy such as the case brought in 2012 by the EU and Japan against Canada on the local content requirements that the province of Ontario attached to its feed-in tariff for the entry of renewables into the electricity grid. Countries have also begun challenging each other's alleged subsidies in the promotion of renewable energy. Some have labelled this a renewable energy trade war, or a trade war in the context of the green economy – wars in which countries want to beat each other to the renewable energy finish line by pouring subsidies into their promotion.

To be confronted with these disputes is far from ideal for the WTO. What the international community needs is the development of stronger, more robust, international energy – and climate – accords that would settle questions such as the ones being brought to the WTO for adjudication. The WTO could then adapt its norms to take account of these international decisions rather than find itself being used as a hammer to shape them by judicial force, a lengthy and confrontational process. But at present, these accords are nowhere to be found, and all we are left with is the risk of trade wars. An alternative could be the negotiation of a WTO agreement on energy, along the lines of other sector accords, such as the WTO Agreement on Agriculture.

Trade negotiations can strengthen WTO contribution

In the Doha Round, energy is being specifically dealt with in the negotiations on services. It is the first time that energy has been discussed as a specific services sector. The negotiations on energy services cover a broad range of activities relevant for energy companies and span all energy sources, including renewables. Commitments are sought on activities such as drilling, engineering, technical testing, construction work for long distance and local pipelines, and more. The negotiations are also addressing the establishment of offices and subsidiaries in third countries, as well as making it easier for specialists and professionals to be transferred within energy services companies. Some WTO members have also proposed negotiating additional disciplines to address, for instance, regulatory transparency, non-discriminatory third-party access to networks and grids, the need for an independent regulator and requirements preventing certain anti-competitive practices.

A second area of the Doha Round relevant to energy relates to clean technology, as we have seen in Chapter 4. The Round aims at opening markets to environmental goods and services. Many of these have a direct application for promoting energy efficiency, such as materials needed for the production of renewable energy, heat management and pollution control.

Similarly, the negotiations on environmental services include negotiations on energy-relevant activities, such as services to reduce exhaust gases and improve air quality, nature and landscape protection services or services for the rehabilitation of mining sites. The environmental chapter of the Round can therefore make a very concrete contribution to the promotion of energy-efficient technologies.

The negotiations on 'trade facilitation' (see Chapter 3) provide a third area. Here, WTO members have been discussing possible improvements to, and clarification of, the GATT 'transit' obligation under which members must allow passage of goods across their territories. In the Round, proposals have been put forward to clarify the meaning of this obligation and whether it includes fixed installations, such as pipelines, which were not an issue when the obligation was drafted in 1947.

Energy-related concerns also underlie proposals on export taxes and subsidies. There are proposals on the table addressing export restrictions on energy goods and other raw materials because these restrictions are more prevalent than in other traded goods and represent a source of concern for importing countries, as they increase prices of inputs. The question of subsidies in the form of low-priced energy products, especially natural gas, has been a recurrent theme of hot debate among WTO members and is also part of the ongoing negotiations.

The picture would not be complete without a word about biofuels. While biofuels can provide us with an opportunity to combat climate change and address energy security and rural development, careful planning is needed to make sure that they do not create new environmental and social problems. For example, the use of corn or sugar cane to produce ethanol has triggered concerns about food security, because it can both limit availability and drive up prices of these food staples. The use of palm oil to generate bio-diesel has led to concerns about deforestation to make way for the planting of palm trees. The negotiations to cut tariffs and discipline agriculture subsidies have the potential to contribute to the development of orderly trade in biofuels. Limiting subsidies for corn feedstock used for ethanol production could lead to a more efficient use of corn.

A more sophisticated WTO rulebook could actually take us closer to all these goals. Having said that, trade policy would still need to be couched in terms of many other accompanying policies, in both the social and environmental spheres. For instance, it is not the rulebook of international trade that will decide how energy gets distributed within a country or settle the ownership of natural resources. Nor is it the WTO rulebook that will ensure that environmental regulations are put in place. The need for accompanying policies and coherence will remain.

As climate change concerns loom ever larger, the WTO could play a role in managing so-called 'leakage', which is the transfer of polluting industries from countries with stringent controls on carbon emissions to those where controls are lighter. It could also address competitiveness concerns arising from the costs of carbon constraints on production. The potential development of international trade in carbon emission permits and the establishment of carbon-offset arrangements, which could be considered subsidies, may also involve a WTO angle. When thinking about how the WTO can most effectively contribute to the energy goals of the international community, the question is not whether the existing WTO framework is relevant and applicable to trade in energy goods and services, for it clearly is. Instead, we need to ask ourselves how the WTO's contribution can be further improved, given rapid changes in the energy policy landscape and the international community's goals regarding energy.

Energy is of fundamental importance to every economy in the world, and to global governance. More predictable and transparent trade rules could benefit both energy-importing and energy-exporting countries, and, beyond them, companies engaged in energy trade and consumers – that is all of us. Market forces can play an important role in the optimal allocation of scarce energy resources and in promoting technological improvements, but, as we have seen, they have their limits when applied to the energy sector.

Better and fairer energy trade rules would help counter temptations towards energy nationalism and prevent conflicts. The WTO has an undeniable role to play in the governance of the evolving energy landscape; it can nurture the energy co-operation between energy-producing and consuming countries that is necessary for our sustainable development. But that role needs to be defined with greater clarity.

9

Trade and currencies: trading community seeks greater currency stability

Exchange rates are, and have always been, a highly sensitive subject in the WTO. There is an emotional, cultural – if not moral – dimension attached to them by the trade community in which the line between reality and perception can become blurred. This is in part because the WTO community has a limited grasp of the workings of the financial system and of the macroeconomic developments that determine exchange rates, such as domestic interest rates and the competitiveness of domestic industry. It is also because, as exchange rates are exogenous to the trade community, some may feel that they are systematically on the receiving end of unwarranted fluctuations. At the start of the financial crisis, in September 2010, the Brazilian Finance Minister, Guido Mantega, cried murder: exchange rate fluctuations were leading to currency wars.

The liberalization of capital flows in the last two decades and the enormous increase in the scale of cross-border financial transactions have increased exchange rate movements. The uncertainty associated with some erratic movements can be not only a source of frustration but also of asymmetric costs, which can distort international competition. Think about the abruptness of local financial crises and how short-term capital flights may spill over into brutal adjustment of exchange rates – a phenomenon observed during the Asian financial crisis of the late 1990s. For small or medium-sized economies, these are enormous shocks to absorb.

The Asian financial crisis of 1997–1998 triggered sharp falls in economic output across the region, along with currency devaluations that bankrupted many companies that had borrowed heavily in foreign currencies. The worst-hit countries had to seek help from the IMF, which is always a politically difficult step for any country to take.

The recent global financial crisis has left WTO members with the vivid sense that the financial sector adjustment in rich economies is destructive for real economies, including those of poorer countries. Exchange rates are perceived to have been a transmission channel for these shocks in several ways. For example, the banking crisis in advanced economies led to a period of slow growth. The slower growth in these countries translated into a weakening of their currencies. This has the effect of making developing countries' exports to these countries more expensive and hence less competitive.

Moreover, advanced economies reacted to the banking crisis by cutting interest rates to boost banks' liquidity. The lower interest rates made it less attractive for international investors to invest in advanced economies. In search of better returns, money poured into developing countries where interest rates were higher. As a result, the currencies of these developing countries further appreciated, worsening their competitive position. This currency disorder strained trade relations, with countries accusing one another of using exchange rates to gain unfair competitive advantage.

Exchange rate adjustments are not all harmful; in fact, exchange rate movements often correct macroeconomic, financial or current account imbalances. Other domestic and international prices can be volatile, too. Just consider fluctuations in commodity prices. One reason why the global trade community dislikes sharp exchange rate movements is because the time perspective of exchange rate markets is different from that of real economy producers and traders. The latter tend to base their decisions on longer-term parameters, i.e. those governing investment, product development and exports. By contrast, exchange rates can move a lot in a short time and introduce considerable uncertainty into real economy pricing and investment decisions.

This difference in time perspective means that the trading community has a natural preference for stability and predictability in their policy environment. (Nevertheless, one tends to hear more complaints from industries in countries where the currency is appreciating than from those in countries where it is depreciating!) Part of the distrust has been ingrained by history; it comes from the gloom and doom of pre-World War Two developments when exchange rate depreciations were associated with unilateral protectionist responses to economic depression, mass unemployment, the rise of populism and dark political developments.

A 2011 survey by the WTO of published research on the relationship between exchange rates and trade showed that, on average, exchange rate volatility has a negative, even if not very large, impact on trade flows. Exchange rate volatility increases commercial risk, introduces uncertainty costs and can influence decisions on whether or not to enter foreign markets. In other words, volatility may affect resource allocation. The extent of these effects depends on a number of factors, including the existence of hedging instruments, the structure of production (e.g. the prevalence of small firms) and the degree of economic integration across countries. For example, larger exporting firms with the possibility of hedging might be less sensitive to exchange rate fluctuations than smaller firms without access to hedging instruments. The impact of exchange rate fluctuations is also reduced by the presence of imported inputs, which offset the effect of exchange rate changes on the pricing of exports. In a world of global supply chains, with an increasing share of imports in exports, one can guess that traditional effects of currency appreciation and depreciation are in part cushioned, although the needed empirical research is yet to be done.

In addition, empirical studies tend to find that exchange rates have a more significant effect in the case of trade with close neighbours, particularly when economies are highly integrated. For example, a 2004 IMF study clearly indicates that exchange rate volatility within the European Union, before the advent of the euro, had a significant impact on relative prices of members because their economies were very integrated commercially.

Economic fundamentals affect the relationship between exchange rates and trade, namely the price elasticity of each traded product, the country's market share of the product concerned, the product composition of exports and imports, the pricing strategy of importers and exporters, etc. Many of these parameters pull in opposite directions. Smaller, open economies, such as New Zealand and Chile, have to bear the full adjustment of exchange rate changes, relative to less trade-dependent, large economies, because they tend to have a less diversified production and export base and hence are less able to switch to exports with greater price elasticity.

To take this further, a firm that has only one export market and whose export earnings depend on bilateral exchange rates is likely to be more affected than firms that are present in global markets (where upwards and downwards movements of various exchange rates may cancel each other out). Global firms also have the possibility of invoicing in local currency, and the capacity to absorb losses due to exchange rate changes and other factors in profit margins. All in all, the most 'sensitive' firms seem not to be the large ones, but rather the smaller ones. And as it is the larger firms that account for the bulk of international trade, the aggregate impact of exchange rate fluctuations on trade tends to be reduced.

Exchange rate misalignments can be seen as sustained deviations of nominal exchange rates from their equilibrium value, itself a difficult concept to pin down and one that depends on the time horizon being taken. But for the purposes of this discussion, it is enough to say that economic models predict that misalignments will have only short-run effects. The exact impact is not straightforward and depends on the specific characteristics of an economy. The latter include the currency in which domestic producers invoice their products and the structure of trade (for example, the prominence of global production networks).

On the empirical side, the complexity of the relationship between exchange rate misalignments and trade also results in mixed findings – it is not always clear that misalignments change the system of relative prices of an economy, at least long enough and deep enough to be able to shift resources or have quantitative effects. For instance, a currency undervaluation is sometimes found to have a positive impact on exports, but the presence, size and persistence of these effects are not consistent across different studies. These effects, when they exist, are predicted to disappear in the medium to long term, unless some other distortion characterizes the economy.

The policy lessons: a need for greater policy coherence

The problem for business is one of excess exchange rate volatility – i.e. when rates behave in a disorderly way and do not adjust to economic fundamentals. The Bretton Woods system of largely fixed exchange rates provided for orderly adjustments among the major currencies. Until it broke down in 1971–1973, giving way to the system of floating rates that we have today, it provided a sense of organized governance in the international monetary system. This is what we lack today.

The IMF and the GATT were created in response to a lack of co-ordination of economic policies during the Great Economic Depression. They aimed at dealing with trade and exchange rate policies as a matter of common interest, with the introduction of disciplines to avoid competitive devaluations, maintain exchange rate stability, limit balance of payments crises and fight protectionism. The international monetary and trading systems were linked from the outset by a coherent set of rules aimed at the progressive liberalization of trade and payments. According to Article IV of the Articles of Agreement of the IMF, 'each member undertakes to collaborate with the Fund and other members to assure orderly exchange arrangements and to promote a stable system of exchange rates'. GATT Article XV requires members to co-operate with the IMF on questions relating to exchange rates and trade. Members are required not to frustrate the intent of the GATT provisions through exchange actions, nor to undermine the provisions of the IMF Article of Agreements through trade actions.

The GATT provisions reflect two things: (1) the attachment of the trade community to exchange rate stability; (2) the need for that community to ensure that the trading system is not frustrated by the undisciplined use of exchange restrictions or multiple exchange rates. These provisions are still part of the WTO rulebook. However, they have not been interpreted; that is, their implications have not been judicially tested, because members have brought no dispute to the WTO. What they mean today, in a WTO and non-Bretton Woods context, is unclear.

However, the institutional set-up remains very much one of coherence – and not of conflict – between the two systems. A lot of WTO members are of the view that stronger disciplines on exchange rates should be implemented in the IMF, the main institution responsible for exchange rate stability. These disciplines need to be discussed and agreed multilaterally. But they do not believe that calling on a WTO judge for remedy will provide a sustainable solution to what is a lack of effective implementation of IMF disciplines within the IMF.

Since the end of the Bretton Woods system, the trading community has consistently asked for greater exchange rate stability and proper adjustments of payments imbalances. This was the case in the 1973 ministerial declaration at the opening of the GATT Tokyo Round and still was in

1994, twenty years later, in the declaration on the 'Contribution of the WTO to Greater Coherence in Global Economic Policy Making', issued at the conclusion of the Uruguay Round.

Reading the 1994 text again, I am struck by the authors' wisdom. It emphasizes on the one hand that 'greater exchange rate stability, based on more orderly underlying economic and financial conditions, should contribute towards the expansion of trade, sustainable growth and development, and the correction of external imbalances'. On the other hand, ministers also 'recognized, however, that difficulties, the origins of which lie outside the trade field, cannot be redressed through measures in the trade field alone'. This says that an international monetary system aimed at greater exchange rate stability and correcting imbalances helps expand trade. At the same time, trade measures cannot correct policy imbalances elsewhere and be an answer to non-trade policy concerns. Tit-for-tat trade measures would be a recipe for protectionist crossfire.

Clearly, erratic exchange rates are an irritant in the trading system. One must acknowledge their influence in trade policy setting, not least because exchange rate shifts may increase or weaken the desired or perceived level of protection of domestic producers. Maintaining multilaterally agreed levels of border protection is certainly a legitimate trade policy objective. The desired levels of protection are negotiated by WTO members through long-term commitments – precisely because policies need to set predictable conditions of access for producers and traders.

At the same time, one may wonder whether long-term levels of protection need to be adjusted to short-term fluctuations or even misalignments of exchange rates. As we have noted, the research literature seems to indicate that exchange rates may have a short-term influence, unless there are substantial market failures, as occurred during the Asian crisis. This raises the question whether long-term border protection should not be considered in the light of the longer-term developments of exchange rates rather than short-term developments.

In general, though, what is needed is an international monetary system that supports cross-border investment and a better allocation of capital across nations, and which 'facilitates international trade' – as laid out in the aims of the IMF. We need a global monetary system that inspires confidence, offers stability and monitors exchange rates more efficiently, one that provides the means to address global imbalances that risk endangering stability.

This is why the international community needs to make headway on the issue of reform of the system, with a view to ensuring greater exchange rate and financial stability. The IMF made a start in 2012 by implementing reform of macroeconomic surveillance, including exchange rates. The reform allows for a more candid assessment by the IMF of deviations of countries' exchange rates relative to equilibrium and their impact on partners' external accounts. It also allows for a better understanding of the spillover effects of domestic macroeconomic policies (fiscal and monetary) of large countries and how they can affect trading partners, notably through exchange rates. This enhanced surveillance allows for more effective 'peer review', an important component of good governance, and should lead eventually to better economic policy co-ordination.

10

Trade and competition: fairer competition makes for fairer trade

On a trip to India in 2010, a senior representative of a local company with global reach complained bitterly to me about how his firm was suffering from unfair and collusive business practices at the hands of its raw material suppliers. Essentially he was accusing his upstream partners – who I won't name – of manipulating supplies and prices to their advantage and his company's cost. What he was complaining about was a classic case of anti-competitive business practice – something that, unfortunately, is far from rare.

As EU Trade Commissioner, I had fought to have negotiations on a competition agreement added to the Doha Round agenda because I believed – as I still believe – that open trade requires fair and transparent policies on competition. But for reasons that will be discussed, developing countries rejected the call at the time and competition policy was, subsequently, excluded from the Round. International trade, however, is changing and, with it, the needs and demands of developing countries, as the case of the businessman from India shows. So the time has come, I would argue, for the WTO to revisit an issue that has important implications for policy coherence and global trade governance.

The link between trade and competition seems obvious: strong policies to promote competition between companies are essential to a dynamic and healthy market economy. Anti-competitive practices, understood as collusive behaviour between firms, or exclusionary practices by a single firm or group of firms, can generate artificial restrictions on imports and exports and raise the prices of agricultural and manufacturing goods and services, thereby eroding the economic gains from trade opening. Economic theory and a wealth of experience demonstrate that effective competition policies help to ensure the efficient allocation of resources in an economy and so provide the best range of choice and supply and the lowest prices for consumers.

It is important, moreover, to note that the 'consumers' affected by anti-competitive practices often are themselves firms – frequently, firms based in developing economies such as that of my Indian friend – that use the products in question as inputs to their own productive activities. So anti-competitive practices directly undermine the competitiveness of these businesses, in both export- and import-competing markets. Yet, the issue of competition has been only briefly debated in the WTO.

What do we mean by competition policy and what sort of practices does it seek to combat? The term is wide-ranging, embracing both domestic legislation and actions of governments and national regulators aimed at preventing anti-competitive abuses, as well as trade policy, both domestic and international. Competition policy seeks to prevent secret understandings between companies and businesses and abusive practices by one or more companies that restrict competition and harm consumers. Collusion may involve attempts to fix prices, limit market access, control supplies, rig bids or any other action that prevents the fair functioning of market forces. Cartels, oligopolies or monopolies are some of the vehicles used by companies to achieve or abuse a position of market dominance and so manipulate business conditions and prices to the benefit of their profits and the detriment of consumers. For open trade, a level playing field inside a country can be just as important as tariff cuts at the border.

Cartels and market-sharing agreements between firms can occur in a single country or across two or more. Economists refer to both as 'horizontal' restraints. Competition is constrained, prices may be inflated, output can be limited and markets may be shared out for the benefit of participating firms. Another form of inter-firm agreement that potentially affects competition, known as 'vertical' restraint, involves restrictive arrangements between companies along a distribution line of products – for example, between the producers of raw materials and those further up the chain who process them.

In all cases, the intention is to promote the interests of the company, or companies, at the expense of the consumer, whether the consumer is an individual or another firm. As tariff barriers fall, thanks to multilateral negotiations and other trade pacts, it is important that the move towards more open markets is not stymied by trade restrictions and distortions resulting from the malpractice of unscrupulous firms.

Anti-competitive practices are far from new; attempts to manipulate food prices by hoarding, for example, are probably as old as agricultural trade itself. In 1776, Adam Smith wrote: 'People of the same trade seldom meet together, even for merriment and diversion, but the conversation ends in a conspiracy against the public, or in some contrivance to raise prices.' Smith felt that nothing much could be done about this, or rather, that the cost to commercial freedom of any action would be too high. And up until the nineteenth century, governments in general did very little. In fact, many governments and rulers earned handsome fees from the sale of monopolies and other commercial advantages.

Over the course of the nineteenth century, however, as the Industrial Revolution spread, the official stance gradually toughened. One of the most important political and judicial attacks on corporate collusion came with a series of anti-trust laws in the United States, beginning with the Sherman Act of 1890. These acts restricted the formation of cartels and banned other practices regarded as being 'restraints on trade', along with monopolization and the abuse of monopoly power. The new laws were used successfully against price fixing among railway companies and, perhaps most famously, to break up the Standard Oil company of John D. Rockefeller. The latter action earned President Theodore Roosevelt the sobriquet of 'trust-buster'.

Nevertheless, it is mainly in the last thirty years or so that countries beyond Europe, Japan and the United States have introduced anti-trust or competition laws. Today, over a hundred countries, including leading emerging economies such as Brazil, China, India, Mexico and South Africa, in addition to the majority of 'economies in transition' in Eastern Europe and Central Asia, have them. Most of these laws bar competition-restricting horizontal agreements and abuses of market dominance and restrict vertical distribution agreements. Increasingly, competition laws are also controlling mergers and acquisitions to deter the creation of monopolies or oligopolies. However, implementing these laws in a coherent, transparent and economically sensible fashion remains a considerable challenge in an interdependent world. These challenges will not be met without dialogue spanning the respective domains of competition and trade policy.

Competition issues are touched on in a number of WTO agreements, including the Agreement on Trade-Related Intellectual Property Rights (TRIPS), but attempts to forge a specific WTO accord on competition and trade have failed. Competition policy was included in the Havana Charter of 1948, but the relevant chapter of the Charter became a dead letter with the failed launch of the proposed International Trade Organization (see Chapter 7). It took fifty years for trade ministers to return to the issue in a substantive way.

At the first WTO Ministerial Conference in Singapore in 1996, ministers agreed to establish a special WTO Working Group on Competition Policy to examine the relationship between trade and competition policy. A compromise reached in Doha in 2001 stated that negotiations could start in 2003, provided all countries agreed. But at the Cancún ministerial meeting of that year, the required consensus was not achieved. A number of developing countries, in particular those without competition laws, were concerned about taking on more obligations and demanded that the issue be dropped. They said that, with the Doha Round underway, their negotiating capacity was already fully deployed and could not stretch to another issue.

However, with the changes taking place in global trade – the rising role of supply chains and the increasing volatility of international commodity prices – the time has come to review this opposition. The world has moved on since the last time competition was discussed at the WTO. In addition to the proliferation of national competition laws across the developing and emerging world, a huge amount of valuable capacity-building work has been done in this area by the OECD and, very actively, by UNCTAD and the International Competition Network (ICN). The latter is an international body devoted to building consensus and convergence on competition law and its implementation, and its members represent national competition agencies and other organizations.

International co-operation in the field of competition policy has gathered pace and includes the UNCTAD Inter-governmental Group of Experts on Competition Law and Policy and the OECD Competition Committee as well as the ICN. Developing countries are not only much better prepared to deal with the issues involved in a negotiation on competition, but most of them probably also now see it as being in their interest.

The case for multilateral disciplines on competition

The food crises of 2007/2008 and 2011 drew renewed attention to the volatility – defined as excessive fluctuations – of commodity prices. To some extent, such volatility is undoubtedly a function of evolving climate conditions and changing economic fundamentals, including the rapid growth of emerging economies. But it is important for the credibility of the trading system to assess and address the role that anti-competitive practices play. Such practices may well turn out to be a factor in higher food prices.

In his contribution to a report entitled 'Trade, Competition and the Pricing of Commodities', US economist John M. Connor cites concerns regarding cartel behaviour in markets in India, Estonia, Italy, Germany and South Africa, to name a few. Market forces must be allowed to work, but they should work within the context of an appropriate set of laws, policies and institutions. This is vital to maintain the confidence of the world's citizens in globalization and the market economy. The report to which Professor Connor contributed was jointly prepared by the UK Centre for Economic Policy Research (CEPR) and the Indian Consumer Unity & Trust Society (CUTS International) following a CUTS symposium on anti-competitive practices in global markets for primary products, held at the WTO in Geneva in September 2011. In it, another economist, Steve McCorriston, noted that one aspect of the modernized food chain is the tendency towards industry consolidation, as reflected in the number of mergers and acquisitions in the food sector over the last twenty years or so. 'Concerns about competition in commodity and food markets stretch across advanced and developing economies, where departures from competitive market structures can involve private firms or state-sanctioned manipulation of market structure ... where the vertically interlinked nature of commodity and food markets results in a complex sequence of successively oligopolistic markets', he wrote.

The 1990s saw a rash of investigations in many countries into the suspected activities of cartels. Many of the major international cartels uncovered – many of these active in developing country markets – were involved in the food and foodstuffs industry. The best known examples were the cartels working in the market for vitamins, lysine – an essential amino acid widely added to animal feed – and citric acid, which is used to flavour and preserve food and beverages. In the lysine case, five companies from the United States, Japan and South Korea were accused of forming a cartel to raise prices in the US$ 600-million-a-year market for the animal-feed additive. Three executives of the US company Archer Daniels Midland were subsequently sentenced to jail. Total fines paid by the companies convicted in the case amounted to US$ 105 million, a record at the time.

Annual international cartel detections have shot up over the past couple of decades, reflecting the increased number of countries with anti-trust authorities to track them down. Nevertheless, despite the hefty fines levied in the lysine case and many other cases, the penalties imposed are often not high enough to act as an effective deterrent, because of the huge gains that collusive practices can yield. Furthermore, there is an important gap in the policy framework almost everywhere, and that gap concerns export cartels. Export cartels largely escape control because, on the one hand, exporting countries are not hurt by them and have little reason to investigate (in many cases, they are even exempted from the exporting countries' national competition laws) and, on the other, many importing countries are unable to enforce their regulations vis-à-vis international companies. While economists have sometimes sought to justify export cartels on purported efficiency gains, they can be pernicious for the economies of importers.

In his study of an export cartel that he alleged to exist in the world potash market – Canada and Russia together hold over 70 per cent of the world's potash reserves – Professor Frédéric Jenny of the ESSEC Business School in Paris, who is also Chairman of the OECD Committee on Competition Law and Policy, calculated that major importers were forced to pay out hundreds of millions of dollars in excess prices. The countries affected by this cartel were predominantly developing countries with fast-growing populations, such as China and India, which needed to boost food production rapidly. Professor Jenny estimated that the surcharges resulting from this cartel arrangement cost China and India some US$ 1.6 billion each annually. He likened the surcharges to an enforced subsidy being paid by emerging economies to a developed one.

Looking beyond the primary products sector, competition policies interact with both development and the international trading system in many other ways. First, there is an important link between private anti-competitive conduct and government measures. The latter may include anti-competitive subsidies, international commodity agreements, price regulations or monitoring regimes and anti-competitive investment measures that unnecessarily limit entry to markets. It seems unlikely that any one set of tools – i.e. the tools of trade as expressed by the current WTO rule book or those of national competition bodies acting alone – can deal effectively with these issues in isolation.

Take the case of state-owned enterprises (SOEs). They play an important role in some of the world's fastest-growing economies, like Brazil, China, India and Russia, and account for a growing share of world trade. In a recent report – 'State-Owned Enterprises: Trade Effects and Policy Implications' – the OECD noted that some SOEs may enjoy 'government-granted advantages' that are 'incompatible with the principles of the World Trade Organization rules-based multilateral trading system'. Anti-competitive effects can arise from countries' use of SOEs as vehicles for commercial, non-commercial or strategic objectives: these can include the acquiring of know-how and technologies abroad or the securing of control over scarce natural materials, the report said.

In addition, governments may grant state-owned firms subsidies to help them overcome foreign competition. These firms may receive concessionary financing, state-backed guarantees or preferential regulatory treatment: all such assistance or exemptions can hinder market access or affect export competition. WTO subsidy rules generally do not cover the services sector, which, as the OECD noted, has a 'strong SOE presence'.

Second, very important synergies exist between market-opening trade measures in government procurement markets and the enforcement of competition or anti-trust laws. If governments fail to put in place tough measures to address bid rigging, the welfare gains made possible by market-opening measures – facilitated, for example, by the WTO Agreement on Government Procurement (GPA) – will surely be jeopardized. Conversely, opening procurement markets to foreign participants, while certainly not making anti-trust enforcement redundant or unnecessary, can undeniably make collusion between firms more difficult, thereby also making good performance more likely. This seems a fruitful area for collaboration between the relevant international organizations, in particular the OECD, UNCTAD and the ICN, in addition to the WTO.

The third way in which competition policies interact with both development and the international trading system is through the relationship between competition policy and intellectual property (IP) rights. This is already recognized in the WTO TRIPS Agreement, but it merits input and reflection from diverse institutional actors. The TRIPS Agreement itself refers to the harm that may be caused by anticompetitive practices and permits governments to take appropriate remedial measures. 'Appropriate measures, provided that they are consistent with the provisions of this agreement, may be needed to prevent the abuse of intellectual property rights by right-holders or the resort to practices which unreasonably restrain trade or adversely affect the international transfer of technology', it declares.

By way of example, the Agreement lists a number of IP licensing practices that can be considered abusive. These include the use of exclusive grant-back conditions (i.e. requirements that a licensee give back to the licensor any improvements that the former makes to the technology concerned), conditions preventing challenges by a licensee to the validity of the underlying IP rights and 'coercive package licensing' – i.e., requiring that a licensee pay for a combination of technologies when, in fact, only one or two elements of the package may be desired.

But this begs important questions – for example, apart from the practices listed, what other kinds of licensing and IP-related practices are potentially harmful to economic welfare, and what remedies are appropriate for these practices? Arguably, even more important than the particular practices flagged in the TRIPS Agreement are various 'next generation' issues concerning competition policy and IP such as: patent thickets – i.e., clusters of overlapping patents that may render new entry to a market difficult or impossible; anti-competitive settlements between brand-name and generic drug companies in relation to patent infringement suits; and the activities of standard-setting organizations in relation to patented technologies and products.

These practices are undeniably complex and their treatment cannot be resolved by any organization acting in isolation. Rather, they call for joint reflection and deliberation by organizations such as WIPO, the OECD, UNCTAD, the ICN and the WTO, in addition to national competition agencies with experience in this field.

A fourth area of policy interaction brings us back to the subject of international cartels, whether in primary products or other markets. The point here is that, when cartels are permitted to operate, they directly undermine the intended benefits that more open trade can bring in the form of expanded supply, employment gains, lower prices and expanded choices for consumers. Instead, supply, and therefore employment, will be restricted, prices will rise and consumer choice will be reduced.

For this reason, all participants in the world trading system have a stake in ensuring that cartels, abuses of dominance and other harmful anti-competitive practices are not tolerated. Some have even suggested that it would be worthwhile, in the framework of the WTO, to prohibit, in principle, the operation of cartels in international trade. International organizations such as the OECD have recognized the harm that cartels – which the OECD refers to as 'hard core' cartels – can do, and the OECD has drawn up recommendations to combat them. It describes cartels as the 'most egregious violations of competition law. They injure consumers in many countries by raising prices and restricting supply, thus making goods and services completely unavailable to some purchasers and unnecessarily expensive for others.' It urges OECD member states to 'ensure that their competition laws effectively halt and deter hard core cartels by providing for effective sanctions and adequate enforcement procedures and institutions to detect and remedy hard core cartels'.

The foregoing are by no means the only areas of interface that exist between competition policy and the international trading system. Other areas include the effects of vertical market restraints and monopolistic conduct on market access, for example in the services sector. In order to address such practices, the WTO General Agreement on Trade in Services (GATS) includes specific provisions on monopoly suppliers of a service. For example, it obliges members to enter into consultations with a view to eliminating such practices upon request by another member. Another area that certainly has not yet been adequately discussed – as it is a relatively new phenomenon – concerns the implications of competition policy for global supply chains, and vice versa. Competition policy is the oil that global supply chains need to function smoothly, whether it is a question of the raw material inputs to products, the networks that distribute them or the services that facilitate the process.

What might a WTO agreement on competition policy look like?

As to what a WTO agreement on competition policy and/or anti-competitive practices might contain, various possibilities could be considered. At the very least, these would seem to include: first, a clear requirement that participating member governments take measures to deal with anti-competitive practices impacting on their respective markets, for example involving international cartels or abuses of a dominant position; second, application of the WTO cornerstone principles of non-discrimination, transparency and procedural fairness; and third, a clear commitment by members to enhanced support for capacity building and international co-operation in this area.

Provision should also be made for the establishment of a WTO competition committee with a mandate for forward-looking exploration and analysis of issues in this area, for example the erosion of market access due to the joint impact of public and private restraints, or the issue of export cartels. Over time, the committee might also address emerging issues concerning IP and the role of competition policy in supply chains, among others. An overarching concern, to be referred to in the mandate of the committee, could be the identification and prevention of anti-competitive practices harmful to world trade and development.

As WTO Director-General, it was my duty to respect the decisions of the membership, and that included keeping my views to myself on the issue of the role of the WTO in regulating trade and competition. As EU Trade

Commissioner I strongly supported the launch of negotiations on a trade and competition agreement, which I thought would bring benefits to both developed and developing countries. Organizations such as the OECD, UNCTAD and ICN do excellent work in the area of competition, but their role is limited to offering guidelines and recommendations, along with training. They do not have much of a bark and certainly no bite. The world trading system, however, needs both. My view has not changed regarding the benefits of a WTO accord on competition. I am convinced that all members, and in particular the weakest, would benefit from clear multilateral disciplines. It is time to re-start the dialogue within the WTO on the effects of anti-competitive practices and their relationship to the international trading system.

Trade and human rights: a case of misplaced suspicion

One of my most daunting moments as WTO Director-General was the day I received a doctor *honoris causa* from the University of Geneva in 2009 in the company of South Africa's Archbishop Desmond Tutu and former UN Human Rights Commissioner Mary Robinson. Not only was I sharing a distinction with a Nobel Peace Prize laureate and one of the people I most admire, I also had to deliver a speech on the place of human rights in a globalizing world. Globalization and human rights; they are for many a case of chalk and cheese! Hadn't the Peace Prize laureate himself been critical of many aspects of globalization? So it was with some trepidation that I put forward my ideas on the issues, and particularly the issues surrounding human rights and trade, which is the part of globalization that – obviously – most closely concerns the WTO.

Trade and human rights might indeed seem an unusual association of concepts. After all, in the eyes of many, trade is a villain, a symbol of neoliberalism, mercantilism and capitalism; it is the tool through which powerful multinational corporations impose their writ over human beings, impairing social, economic and cultural rights. The history of the relationship between trade and human rights is a history of suspicion and to some extent of deliberate reciprocal ignorance. The WTO has been depicted as a leading instrument of a globalization in which the market takes precedence over individuals and might over right. It was not so long ago that its ministerial meetings drew large, often violent, demonstrations of protest from anti-globalization groups.

But this view of trade, the WTO and human rights is not just simplistic, it is also misguided. Globalization and the opening up of trade can work in favour of universal human rights, understood as civil and political rights as well as economic and social rights. Trade presupposes human interaction, respect and understanding. If conducted with respect, 'trade polishes and softens the most barbarous mores', to quote Montesquieu and his theory of 'doux commerce'.

Trade, however, does not automatically promote the cause of human rights. This requires rules that are both global and just. It requires rules of the kind that prompted Henri-Dominique Lacordaire, the nineteenth-century French ecclesiastic and political activist, to say that 'between the weak and the strong, the poor and the rich ... liberty is the oppressor and the law is freedom'. Negotiating and implementing such just and global rules is the WTO's basic mission, and its primary vocation in so doing is to regulate and not to 'deregulate', as is often thought. By putting in place rules to regulate trade flows and remove trade distortions, the WTO aims to create a level playing field where fairness is the rule and where the rights of individual WTO members are safeguarded. In other words, its mission is to combat the situation depicted by Oxfam International: 'Trade generates incredible wealth, and links the lives of everyone on the planet. However, millions of people in poor countries are losing out because the rules controlling trade heavily favour the rich nations that set the rules.'

One too often forgets that human rights and trade rules, including WTO rules, are based on the same values – individual freedom and responsibility, non-discrimination, rule of law and welfare through peaceful co-operation among individuals. Not only do they derive from the same fundamental values, they are the result of common concerns. Both human rights and global trade rules were considered a key element of the post-World War Two order and a rampart against totalitarianism. It is no coincidence that the seeds of the multilateral trading system were planted at the same time as the Universal Declaration of Human Rights was being drafted in the mid-1940s. Both were seen as indispensable to world peace. 'Those that trade together can live together.' This was the thinking behind the setting up of the European Coal and Steel Community in 1951, just six years after the end of World War Two. The Community eventually evolved into the European Union that we have today. Today it is hard to imagine France and Germany, which fought three brutal wars between 1870 and 1945, again taking up arms against each other.

I would argue that trade and human rights are also linked in another fundamental way. Human rights and trade are mutually supportive. Human rights are essential to the good functioning of the multilateral trading system, and trade and WTO rules contribute to the realization of human rights. What role do human rights play in trade? Civil and political rights are crucial to good governance, which in turn is essential to the proper conduct of trade relations. Freedom of expression, for example, brings transparency, one of the core principles of the world trading system. Social, economic and cultural rights, often proclaimed by critics as the main victims of globalization and of the opening of markets, are in fact important ingredients of successful trade opening in so far as the latter brings economic growth whose rewards are fairly distributed. It is through the extension and deepening of such fundamental rights that the benefits of trade must finally be measured, even though, as we shall see later in this chapter, arriving at such a measurement is not easy.

But what is the place of international trade law in promoting human rights in practice? I would start by noting that trade measures are the instrument most commonly adopted by developed countries to put pressure on states violating human rights. They can be used as either a carrot, in the form of the offer of greater trading opportunities, or as a stick, through the imposition of restrictions, such as embargoes. Examples of the latter include the trade sanctions enforced against South Africa in the mid-1980s in an effort to weaken apartheid. But more importantly, as I have argued throughout this book, trade is a means to an end. Opening international trade can raise living standards and contribute to implementing fundamental human rights. But it does not always work like that.

This is particularly true in the case of those whom Amnesty International calls the 'prisoners of poverty', that is people who are deprived of a host of social and economic rights, such as the right to clean water, the right to health or the right to food. As an example, I would cite Article 11 of the International Covenant on Economic, Social and Cultural Rights, which concerns the right to food and advocates 'taking into account the problems of both food-importing and food-exporting countries, to ensure an equitable distribution of world food supplies in relation to need'. WTO negotiations on the reduction of trade barriers in agriculture, enhanced market access for agricultural products and the gradual decrease in subsidies provided by rich countries to their farmers, for example, all contribute to the same objective – the implementation of the right to food for all (see Chapter 5).

The opening of markets boosts economic efficiency, stimulates growth and helps spur development, so contributing to the achievement of fundamental social and economic rights. One could almost claim that trade is human rights in practice! Of course, trade rules are not perfect. They may, in some cases, have unintended consequences that can threaten human rights. Some claimed this to be the case with respect to intellectual property (IP) rights and access to medicines, as we saw in Chapter 6. These concerns, which were sparked by certain provisions of the TRIPS Agreement, led trade negotiators to amend the accord to facilitate access to affordable medicines for developing countries with no or little domestic pharmaceutical production of their own. Similarly, discussions are underway at the WTO about folklore and traditional knowledge, with the aim of protecting the rights of indigenous people and other groups in matters such as the patenting of medicines that incorporate ingredients or knowledge that these groups developed or use.

Some people have blamed globalization for the Bangladesh garment factory disaster of April 2013 (see Chapter 7). They argue that the pressure on poor developing countries to produce goods cheaply for the mass markets of the rich West is responsible for the lack of worker protection. But it is also true that it is this very same globalization process that has led to the strong international reaction to the tragedy and the pressure for immediate steps to prevent any recurrence in Bangladesh and elsewhere.

Trade can anchor human rights

Jurists debate at length whether the WTO is bound to respect human rights, but for me the answer is a clear 'yes'. Respect for human rights is incumbent on the members of the organization because – as states – they are bound by their international obligations, by their signatures on international treaties and declarations. WTO case law has acknowledged that international trade law cannot be interpreted 'in clinical isolation' from international law in general. And how could the WTO, created by an international legal instrument, be immune to the rules of general international law from which it derives its mission and its very existence?

In fact, I sense a growing awareness among trade experts of the importance of human rights and of the role trade can play in promoting and anchoring such rights. But I say 'can' advisedly, because in my view this is true only in certain conditions that need to be specified and that are far from being fulfilled everywhere. Trade opening can entail social costs. To be successful, the opening of markets requires solid social policies to prevent the excessive concentration of wealth and to provide safety nets for the men and women whose living conditions may have been disrupted by evolving trade rules and trade patterns.

Open trade does not suffice unless it is accompanied by policies designed to correct the imbalances between winners and losers; and the greater the vulnerability of economies, societies or individuals, the more dangerous the imbalances. It does not suffice unless it goes hand in hand with a sustained international effort to help the developing countries to build the capacity they need to take advantage of open markets.

If I had to pinpoint one principle governing the conditions in which globalization and the opening up of trade must help to promote and ensure respect for human rights, I would say that it is coherence. Coherence must be reflected in the political commitment of citizens, of civil society and of trade unions, and in the relationship between the local and the global. Today the world needs more coherence in the organization of government between national and global, more coherence between the different islands making up the archipelago of international governance. In other words, it needs the 'Geneva Consensus' and the policy coherence that we have been discussing in this book.

Today's world may be 'flat', to paraphrase the US journalist and author Thomas Friedman, but it is not united. It is, on the contrary, more fragmented than ever. The wind of globalization, which has been blowing during the past few decades, has dispersed our energies. We need to bring them together and act in a co-ordinated way. We need to build an international order in which, to quote Jean-Jacques Rousseau, 'the stronger is never strong enough to be forever master, unless he transforms his force into right and obedience into duty'. To which Simone Weil added, on a more personal and meditative note: 'It is a duty for every man to uproot himself in order to attain the universal, but it is always a crime to uproot others.'

The logic of increasing market integration demands increasing integration of the social and ethical values that exist alongside it. Take the example of tariffs and border restrictions. Previously, such barriers were designed almost exclusively to protect local producers from external competition. But today, non-tariff barriers, which, as we have seen, are becoming increasingly important in world trade, are intended – at least in theory – to protect consumers, not producers, from a threat to their health and well-being. Food imports are an obvious example, but health and safety regulations apply to a host of goods, including toys and medicines. Environmental protection is another important reason invoked for deploying non-tariff barriers. But the norms, regulations and standards, on which the non-tariff measures draw, are established according to scales or degrees of perceived risk that are not ethically neutral.

Any risk calculation involves a judgement about what is good and what is bad, or at least about what is better or what is worse. The precautionary principle that we met in Chapter 6 on health, which is essentially what we are talking about here, rests upon the ethical or social values of a community. Where these values differ, they can become a barrier to the free exchange of goods, with producers being obliged to take account of different standards in different markets. In so far as these differences erase economies of scale, they negate one of the big economic advantages of globalization. Global market integration, therefore, requires convergence and the harmonization of the value systems that underpin the precautionary principle. We have an example of such harmonization in the creation of the single market within the European Union during the 1990s.

153

But achieving such harmonization on a global scale will be far from easy. We have already seen in our discussion on labour standards how many countries oppose the mixing of social and labour standards with trade. As the tragedy in Bangladesh shows, it may be hard to reach a clear and objective scale on which to weigh poverty reduction and worker protection and come out with an ethical and moral balance that satisfies all. Market capitalism will always give greater weight to the standardization of objects and goods rather than human rights. It is one of its defects. And we cannot even rely on science when it comes to the precautionary principle, as the arguments over genetically modified foods show. Science may indicate a certain conclusion, but this may not suffice to satisfy consumers and hence the politicians who make the rules.

Fair trade movements and organizations attempt to reconcile trade and ethics or trade and social and environmental sustainability. From coffee to flowers, there are organizations that certify that these goods have been produced in a way that meets certain moral and ecological standards. But beyond the core ILO standards we mentioned in Chapter 6, there is no internationally accepted definition of fairness when it comes to working conditions. So how do we assess what is fair and what is not? As a matter of fact, the notion of fair trade, and the accompanying proliferation of private standards of an ethical nature, is regarded by some as disguised protectionism and therefore by no means 'fair'. Fair trade, while certainly not an oxymoron, is a difficult concept to pin down and will remain so as long as all parties to commerce do not agree on a definition of the term. But that does not mean that we should not strive for such a definition. However, this definition cannot be unilateral. After all, fair trade is what participants to trade agree is fair. Finding that agreement, however, is complicated by the lack of any global forum in which to discuss it.

Human rights are '*jus cogens*' – norms that cannot be transgressed – and are accepted as such by the entire international community. It is within this universal framework that the contribution of trade opening to the promotion of human rights can and must find its place both in law and in practice. The responsibility lies with all of us. It is the responsibility of the members of the WTO, which are practically all party to either the International Covenant on Civil and Political Rights or the International Covenant on Economic, Social and Cultural Rights, to uphold their human rights obligations while complying with the organization's trade rules.

But it is also the responsibility of the WTO, of the Office of the High Commissioner for Human Rights – which is the custodian of human rights treaties – and of organizations such as the International Council on Human Rights and Realizing Rights to work to co-ordinate their actions in a meaningful and efficient manner to ensure that trade does not impair human rights, but rather strengthens them. I am aware of the challenge this represents, of the change in mindset this requires. My own modest attempts to bridge the trade and human rights communities have raised eyebrows in both circles; chalk is chalk and Camembert is Camembert.

12

Corruption: a cancer that trade transparency can help to treat

On a recent visit to Ghana, I was shown a map of trade corridors in West Africa indicating the level of bribes that truck drivers are required to pay and the resulting delays. Compiled by the West African Economic and Monetary Union, with assistance from USAID, the numbers are eloquent: in Burkina Faso, a truck driver pays on average more than US$ 50 in bribes and loses more than 70 minutes every 100 km! Corruption certainly takes its toll on efficiency and on the cost of doing business.

The West Africa Trade Hub initiative was launched in 2006. Trained drivers voluntarily collect data as they load goods from ports in Ghana, the Ivory Coast, Senegal and Togo and transport them to the capitals of landlocked Burkina Faso and Mali. Detailed reports on the extent of corruption and the resulting delays are published quarterly. By increasing transparency, the initiative aims to promote good governance on West Africa's trade corridors.

Bribery and corruption are of course not limited to certain countries or regions and certainly not to Africa. No country is immune. It is a global issue, and a major concern, not only for victims of corrupt practices, but also for the world at large. According to Gallup's Global NGO barometer, corruption is widely regarded as a bigger problem than economic issues.

Corruption can take various forms, from bribery to embezzlement, where a person in a position of trust, such as an agent, illegally exploits that trust, and even nepotism. As the West Africa initiative shows, trade offers opportunities for corruption but is also a victim of corruption. It is difficult to know how much international trade is affected but if corruption represents only 1 per cent of world trade, it would mean US$ 200 billion per year. Not a small sum . . .

During my eight years at the head of the WTO, I was often asked whether the organization could not help to tackle corruption. My view is that it already does to a certain extent but more could be done.

The WTO and the fight against corruption

The WTO has no trade rule that directly addresses corruption and it has no negotiating mandate or work programme on corruption. WTO agreements, however, contain a number of obligations that can help to tackle corruption.

One way is to have greater transparency. As the old saying goes, 'sunshine is the best disinfectant'! This is where Transparency International has a role to play. Founded in 1993 by Peter Eigen, a former World Bank official, it regularly publishes a 'Corruption Perceptions Index' and a 'Bribe Payers Index', which help to raise the public profile of corruption and to place it on the radar screens of corporate and political leaders. I was one of the founders of the French 'chapter' at the end of the 1990s and I have been closely associated with it ever since.

As the West Africa Trade Hub initiative has shown, publishing numbers on corruption puts pressure on governments. It is an important form of transparency, which is of course at the core of the WTO's mandate.

WTO rules contribute to better transparency in four ways. First, they require WTO members to promptly publish laws, regulations, judicial decisions and administrative rulings before they enter into force. Secondly, they require WTO members to notify new trade measures to the WTO if these measures will affect other members. Thirdly, they task members to establish enquiry points that can answer questions from other countries about issues such as sanitary and phytosanitary measures, relating to food safety and animal/plant health, or technical barriers to trade. Finally, the WTO conducts regular reviews of individual countries' trade policies and practices.

But sanctions for not complying with these rules are rare. A country's failure to promptly publish laws and regulations affecting trade has been invoked in only a couple of cases by the WTO's dispute settlement panels to support a ruling that measures have violated WTO rules.

Another important way of curbing corruption is to reduce the use of non-tariff trade measures which are increasingly becoming the main obstacle to trade as the levels of tariffs decline worldwide. Many WTO agreements aim to reduce the arbitrary nature of such measures relating to issues such as car emission limits, product and food safety standards or customs procedures.

A good example of non-tariff measures is pre-shipment inspection, which expanded significantly in the

THE FIGHT AGAINST CORRUPTION

1980s. This involves employing private companies to check shipment details of export goods – essentially price, quantity and quality – to ensure that the value of shipments is not understated and to prevent capital flight, commercial fraud and the avoidance of customs duties. Although intended to reduce tariff fraud, such procedures can be used by officials to obtain illicit payments in exchange for accelerating procedures or altering the inspector's decision.

During the Uruguay Round of trade negotiations, a specific agreement was negotiated to help reduce the arbitrary nature of pre-shipment procedures. The agreement stipulates that inspection be carried out within five working days. This time frame is intended to limit opportunities for corruption. The agreement also includes provisions to prevent over-invoicing or under-invoicing and fraud.

Another agreement that aims to reduce corruption is the WTO agreement on import licensing. Under import licensing procedures, an importer is required to submit an application before importing goods. It does not require a great stretch of the imagination to see how such procedures could give rise to abuse and corruption.

The WTO Agreement on Import Licensing Procedures aims to ease the process of applying for licences and to limit the scope for arbitrary decisions. To make the licensing process simple, transparent and predictable, it requires governments to publish information that allows traders to understand the basis for granting and allocating licences. It describes how countries should notify the WTO when they introduce new licensing procedures or change existing arrangements and offers guidance on how governments should assess applications for licences. Although important, these provisions remain modest.

The most stringent agreement tackling potential corruption is the WTO Agreement on Government Procurement. This agreement regulates the purchase by governments of goods and services from private enterprises for use in the public sector. Throughout history, government procurement has been a fertile soil for corrupt practices. The amounts at stake are usually high, making it tempting for an official to take a percentage of the transaction costs. The procurement market is believed to represent 10 to 15 per cent of a country's GDP – Transparency International even estimates it to be 15 to 30 per cent. This is not surprising, as in most countries the government and its agencies are the biggest purchasers of all types of goods, ranging from office furniture to high-tech equipment.

The WTO Government Procurement Agreement entered into force in 1981. Its purpose is to open up government procurement as much as possible to international competition. It aims to make laws, regulations, procedures and practices regarding government procurement more transparent and to ensure they do not discriminate against foreign products or suppliers. Ensuring open, transparent and non-discriminatory procurement practices is essential for achieving 'value for money', particularly at a time of huge financial constraints for public budgets.

Currently, forty-three WTO members are party to the Government Procurement Agreement and several other members, including China, are in the process of negotiating their accession to it. A revised version of the agreement, adopted in March 2012, marked a milestone by creating an explicit link between the WTO and tackling corruption. The preamble to the agreement states: 'recognizing the importance of transparent measures regarding government procurement, of carrying out procurements in a transparent and impartial manner and of avoiding conflicts of interest and corrupt practices, in accordance with applicable international instruments, such as the United Nations Convention against Corruption.' This is the first time that the word 'corruption' has appeared in a WTO agreement.

The revised procurement agreement includes specific provisions to prevent corrupt practices and makes it possible for a party to the agreement to exclude a supplier on grounds such as 'final judgments in respect of serious crimes or other serious offences' or 'professional misconduct or acts or omissions that adversely reflect on the commercial integrity of the supplier'.

These examples show that the WTO has a role to play in fighting corruption, but could it do more? Could its role be reinforced? This is of course for WTO members to decide, but I believe that more could be done.

Towards a greater role for the WTO

WTO members are currently negotiating ways of improving customs procedures. The stakes are high: UNCTAD estimates that the average customs transaction involves 20 to 30 different parties, 40 documents, 200 types of data and the re-keying of 60–70 per cent of all data at least once. The number of parties involved obviously leads to a higher risk of corruption. An agreement on trade facilitation – as it is called in WTO jargon – would simplify customs procedures and improve transparency. It would help reduce the administrative 'thickness' of borders and curb corrupt practices. The OECD estimates that the gains from introducing trade facilitation measures could be as much as 10 per cent of trade costs in developed countries and between 13 and 15 per cent in developing countries.

In the longer term, there could even be a specific WTO anti-corruption agreement. Admittedly, this would be delicate to negotiate, but it has been suggested by some. The panel of experts that I convened in 2012 to consider the future of trade reported that in the course of its consultations many individuals expressed concerns about widespread corruption and its impact on economies and trade. Many of these individuals advocated a stronger role for the WTO in the fight against corruption. Why the WTO and not other organizations, such as the UN Convention against Corruption or the OECD with its Anti-Bribery Convention? Because the WTO is the only international organization that has a binding dispute settlement system. It is the only organization whose rules are truly enforceable.

Negotiating specific rules on corruption in the framework of the WTO would not be easy. It would require long, meticulous preparations – I am not even talking here about a potential outcome. The launch of such negotiations would require a mandate. Ideally, such a mandate should stem from a group of WTO members that is representative of the membership and that brings together both developed and developing countries. The aims for the agreement would have to be carefully calibrated to avoid ambiguity and stalemate. Support from the G20 major economies would also help.

Work is already under way within the G20 Anti-Corruption Group, established at the G20 Toronto Summit in 2010. G20 leaders endorsed the first Anti-Corruption Action Plan later that year, in Seoul. The first monitoring report was published under the French presidency in 2011 – a report to which the WTO contributed, along with other international organizations, such as the World Bank, the International Monetary Fund, the OECD and the United Nations Office on Drugs and Crime (UNODC). Work has been proceeding under the Russian presidency, with inputs from the B20 (businesses), C20 (civil society) and the L20 (trade unions).

So maybe things are moving forward. The road ahead will be long and bumpy – but looking at the West African map and listening to business people around the world, it is plain to see how long and bumpy it already is! With political will, careful planning, good support and effective co-ordination between the various stakeholders and organizations involved, I believe we can work together to help cure the cancer of corruption by establishing global binding disciplines.

13

Last but not least: the Doha Round

This book is laced with references to the Doha Round and its importance for the global economy and the multilateral trading system. The Round – the run-up, the launch, the negotiations – was a fundamental part of my professional life for nearly fifteen years, first as EU Trade Commissioner and then as WTO Director-General. I think I can safely say that I know it better than almost anyone, better probably than anyone would want to know it. So what has happened, and perhaps more importantly, what should happen to bring finally the long-running saga to a close?

Let's begin by reaffirming why the Doha Round – also known as the Doha Development Agenda – was and is needed. WTO rules were last updated in 1995 and it is clear that the existing regulations are both unfair and increasingly outdated. It is inequitable that the rules permit countries to pour billions of dollars into agriculture programmes in the form of subsidies, subsidies that have impoverished developing country farmers over the last three decades by making it difficult for them to compete on world markets. It is unjust that the WTO tariff system allows countries to hit exports from poor countries with duties three or four times higher than those applied to exports from wealthier countries. It is impossible to keep providing subsidies which contribute to overfishing our oceans.

But it also makes little sense that trade rules should focus so heavily on tariffs, which have fallen over the years to average little over 5 per cent worldwide, while saying little about mushrooming non-tariff barriers such as technical standards. While global value chains are transforming the architecture of trade, invalidating some traditional mercantilist assumptions, rules on the movement of goods through customs date back to a time before bar coding and laptops. It also makes little sense, at a time when South–South trade represents almost one-third of world trade, to keep barriers to trade high between developing countries.

At the same time there has been an upheaval in the power structure of global trade. When the Doha Round was launched in November 2001, China was not a member of the WTO and Brazil, India and a number of other developing countries had yet to emerge as global economic players. The so-called North, the developed countries, still dominated global trade in terms of volume and value. But in the past decade or so, the situation has changed dramatically, with trade between developing countries surging to become an increasingly important component of global commerce (see Chapter 2). All these factors influence the negotiations and their chances of success.

Successful completion of the Doha Round would bring big progress in reducing tariffs, both agricultural and industrial, addressing tariff peaks (that is, exceptionally high tariffs on selected products) and tariff escalation. This is the practice of setting higher import duties on semi-processed and finished products than on raw materials, thus discouraging the development of processing activity in the countries where raw materials originate.

Conclusion of the Doha Round would make substantial inroads into addressing those trade-distorting subsidies in agriculture and the environmentally damaging subsidies for fishing, and open up trade in services, which, as we have seen, is a vital part of global trade. It would mark a step forward in tackling some non-tariff measures, which have emerged as probably the biggest barrier to trade in both goods and services, and haul customs practices into the computer era, saving billions of dollars of unnecessary costs along the way.

The hard fact is that wrapping up the Round is difficult precisely because its results will be meaningful: this round is two or three times greater than the Uruguay Round in terms of cuts in tariffs and subsidies and in commitments. Also this is a true 'development round' that lives up to its billing in that not only would developing countries benefit from more open trade, but trade opening by all WTO members would contribute to development. If measured in terms of duties forgone, two-thirds of the potential benefits of tariff and subsidy cuts resulting from the Round will accrue to developing countries' exports. In sum, if and when it is concluded, the multilateral trading system will be more open – particularly for developing countries' exports – and will have a strengthened rule-making structure that will make it more balanced, especially towards developing-country interests and concerns. A successful conclusion would, therefore, further help poorer developing countries in their quest to meet the Millennium Development Goals (MDGs), in particular their fight to alleviate poverty.

A further big prize would be the certainty, predictability and stability it would bring to global trade. It is in a moment of economic crisis, such as the prolonged one that began in 2008, that the value of this insurance policy increases. The pressures on governments for protectionist actions rose as the crisis continued. They showed up in the regular monitoring exercises carried out in the WTO, and they were worrying. To turn to protectionist trade measures in these circumstances would be a huge mistake – one that could send the global economy back into deep recession. The undisputed contribution that market opening and the maintenance of open markets – on the basis of global rules – has made to growth and greater prosperity in so many countries in the post-World War Two period ought to have been sufficient to convince governments and the public of the need for continuing trade co-operation.

But we all know that things are not that simple. Governments feel short-term pressures to take what seem like expedient actions in favour of domestic production, forgetting not only the domestic consequences of such actions for efficiency and productivity in the domestic economy, but also the likelihood of being repaid in kind by trading partners. It is understandable that at a time of suffering we all run for shelter. We want protection. But the irony is that trade protectionism does not protect. One country's exports are another country's imports, and vice versa. It is particularly pointless in a world in which the import content of exports is already over 40 per cent. One country's protectionism will lead to another country's protectionism. And everyone will lose, as happened in the aftermath of the Great Depression in the 1930s. As Gandhi said, 'an eye for an eye and we will all be blind'.

We are at a stage in trade relations where we need to see a practical reaffirmation from governments of their commitment to international trade co-operation and the

institutional arrangements that support the multilateral
trading system. If we do not reaffirm this commitment with
more than words, especially now that the going has got tough,
we risk letting things get to a point where it becomes harder
to pull back from a path of continuing deterioration. By
improving the credibility of the WTO, by ensuring it keeps
moving forward, its members would contribute towards
restoring global stability and predictability. A more open,
fairer and more development-friendly trading system is part
of the solution to the global economic crisis. Exiting crises is
easier if it is done in a spirit of global co-operation, and part
of that co-operation in this case involves achieving a global
trade deal.

To achieve it, we will need to recapture the sense of
commitment and solidarity of November 2001 when, two
months after the chilling terrorist attacks on New York, world
leaders agreed to launch the Doha Round. They did so out of
a realization that a significant gesture of international unity
was needed to reassure an anxious public and restore confidence in a shaken global economy. Some WTO members,
notably the United States and the European Union, had
begun pressing for a new round almost before the ink was
dry on the Uruguay Round negotiations. They tried and failed
at the WTO ministerial conference in Seattle in 1999, and
without September 11, they would probably have failed again
in Doha.

The other great incentive for accepting a new round –
at least on the part of poorer developing countries who were
initially the most sceptical – was the pledge to put development at its heart. Some felt that calling the Doha Round the

Doha Development Agenda was a mistake. Not only might it raise false expectations, because the WTO is not a development agency, but it might give the impression that developing countries would not have to concede anything in the negotiations. I did not and do not accept either argument. By calling it a 'development round', the WTO acknowledged the fact that two-thirds of its members are developing countries and that many of the anomalies in its global rules of trade are there because the rules were written mainly by developed countries. The new round was going to correct many of these anomalies in the name of development. But equally importantly, by calling it a development round, WTO members were also signalling clearly their conviction that, by preparing the ground for more open trade by all, they would be contributing to development.

The objective of the Doha Round is to improve the multilateral disciplines and the commitments by all members of the WTO in such a way that they establish a more level playing field and provide developing countries with better conditions to enable them to reap the benefits of opening trade. Let's take an example of what was happening with tariffs. In January 1996, the US imported US$ 3 billion worth of French goods – and collected roughly US$ 30 million in import tariffs. In the same month, the US imported only US$ 200 million worth of goods from Cambodia – that is less than 10 per cent of US imports from France – but the amount of import duties paid was the same – US$ 30 million! The nub of the problem is the type of goods that each country exports. Today, if a country exports low value-added products, like textiles, clothing and footwear – usually produced by poor countries – it pays high duties. This situation must be changed, and concluding this round can do it.

A difficult start

The negotiations were never going to be easy – there is a lot at stake – and they quickly ran into trouble. I attended the Cancún ministerial conference of 2003, the first to follow the launch of the Doha Round, in my then capacity as EU Trade Commissioner. The meeting ended in bitter deadlock, with no agreement on the key issues on the table. The visible stumbling bloc in Cancún was whether some contentious areas of the negotiations, including new rules for policies on competition and investment, should be dropped from the Doha Round. As EU Trade Commissioner, I fought unsuccessfully to keep them in, and I think time has shown those of us who backed their inclusion were right. Were these issues still on the agenda, it might be easier to find the sort of trade-offs needed to conclude the Round. At the same time, competition and investment issues have become increasingly important in world trade and their absence from the negotiations will leave a big gap in global trade governance.

This was the visible obstacle – the obstacle that featured most in press coverage of the collapse of the Cancún talks. But the other big obstacle, the one that was more hidden, was cotton. Cotton had become a prominent issue in the run-up to Cancún. Four West African cotton-producing countries had written to the then WTO Director-General, Supachai Panitchpakdi, calling for cotton to be given special treatment in the agricultural negotiations. The four countries – Benin, Burkina Faso, Chad and Mali – called for an end to production subsidies in rich countries, particularly the United States. They also wanted to be compensated for lost earnings because they saw the subsidies as preventing them from competing on world markets. But a proposal by Supachai and the chairman of the conference, Mexican Foreign Minister Luis Ernesto Derbez, was angrily rejected by the Africans as being too favourable to the United States. The chances of an accord on cotton were not helped by the heavy presence in Cancún of US cotton lobbyists, who were constantly pressuring US Trade Representative Bob Zoellick.

But Cancún did see the creation of two new developing-country negotiating groups, the G20 and the G90. The G20, which is not to be confused with the G20 financial grouping of leading developed and developing states, was formed on Brazil's initiative and brought together major developing-country exporters of agricultural goods. Brazil saw it forming a counterweight to the US and the EU on agricultural issues. The creation of the G20 led to the birth of the G90. The G90 group brought together developing countries with more defensive agricultural interests. These were countries, many of them former colonies, which feared that they could lose preferential trade deals with rich countries if farm trade barriers came down too quickly.

Cancún was a frustrating experience; so frustrating, in fact, that at my closing press conference, I branded the WTO's way of working as 'medieval'. The term delighted journalists but came back to haunt me somewhat when – two years later – I became a candidate to lead the organization.

But as is often the way in the stop–go process of multilateral negotiations, the setback in Cancún gave way months later to a period of greater optimism. In July 2004 ministers agreed a set of measures – the so-called 'July package' – that for a time seemed to put the negotiating train back on the rails. The package was largely based on a deal struck previously between myself, in the name of the EU, and the then US Trade Representative Bob Zoellick. Under the 'framework', as it was called, the EU agreed to a deadline for abolishing export subsidies for agricultural goods, the US accepted deeper cuts in farm production subsidies, some special measures were finally approved to help African cotton producers and guidelines were fixed for opening up trade in manufactured goods. Members also agreed to launch negotiations on trade facilitation (see Chapter 3). Despite the fact that the initial 1 January 2005 deadline for concluding the Round was missed, the stage really seemed finally set for progress.

The momentum was maintained into 2005. At the Hong Kong ministerial conference at the end of the year, trade ministers added services to the July framework and reached an accord on duty-free and quota-free access for exports from least-developed countries (LDCs). When the ministerial declaration was gavelled shortly before Christmas of 2005, it fuelled hopes that 2006 could see a definitive breakthrough. But it was not to be.

In 2006, trade ministers, meeting in Geneva, tried but failed to agree a draft accord, a blueprint for an eventual Doha deal. Nobody was prepared to make the necessary concessions: the United States baulked at offering further cuts in agricultural subsidies, the European Union at dropping import barriers to farm goods, and the big developing countries – India and Brazil – at opening up their markets further for industrial goods. Faced with the impasse, the only thing I could do, as Director-General, was to recommend the suspension of negotiations across the Round to give a time-out to review the situation, examine available options and review positions.

The next big push came in 2008, again in Geneva. This time trade ministers came very close to approving draft deals in agriculture and industrial goods that would have provided the springboard for agreement across the Doha agenda. Agreement was achieved on something like seventeen of the twenty topics on the agenda. But we hit the wall on a technical matter – how to provide specific safeguards to poor country farmers when agriculture imports rise suddenly. What were the acceptable thresholds for import surges and what level of tariff protection could be applied – known as 'safeguards' in WTO-speak? Some countries, including India, Indonesia, the Philippines and China, believed existing agreements did not yield sufficient safeguard protection for their millions of poor farmers, who could suffer if food imports were allowed suddenly to rise. Others, including the United States, Uruguay, Thailand and Paraguay, found it difficult to accept that a negotiation designed to bring trade barriers down could result in some existing tariffs going up.

I felt the failure of the 2008 talks deeply. For the first time, the WTO had authorized the Director-General to take the initiative and draft a personal proposal for a possible compromise deal in agriculture and industrial goods.

The one-page plan I produced ahead of the ministerial meeting, which included the contentious safeguards issue, was accepted by virtually everybody, including the EU, Brazil and China.

Only India said 'no' outright, with the Americans being at first non-committal. But this opening hard line by the Indians reflected a belief that, when it came to it, the Americans would not accept a deal. And they were proved right. With presidential elections due in the autumn of 2008, the US administration was not prepared to take the risk and accept an agreement that could upset the farm and other lobbies back home. So when the Indians subsequently appeared to give some ground, the Americans dug in and refused any further compromise. But before this point, the mood had clearly swung from sceptical to enthusiastic. Many issues, which until then had been unattractive, found accommodation: how to treat products where preferential treatment in EU and US markets would be eroded, or how to give greater liberalization to 'tropical agricultural products'. Even the long-standing banana issue between the EU and a group of Latin American countries found a path to resolution, and would finally be resolved in 2012.

The ministerial meeting had been tense, marked by late-night sessions and frayed nerves, but there were also some colourful moments. At one long negotiating session, India's Trade Minister Kamal Nath berated the United States for what he said was its refusal to cut 'even one dollar' from its farm subsidies. Finally, US Trade Representative Susan Schwab turned round to an aide and asked for the loan of a dollar bill which she then handed to Nath saying, 'Here's your dollar'.

On the final night, using the usual WTO approach of varying the negotiating format, I gathered together just four key players – the United States, the European Union, Brazil and India – in a bid to break the deadlock. The Japanese trade minister insisted on waiting outside the room, keen to join the talks at the first opportunity. But as the discussions dragged on, the minister became more and more agitated. Finally, I was forced to go out to speak to him. I was met by a verbal tirade, first from the minister, in Japanese, and then from his interpreter, who felt obliged to imitate the gestures and the raised voice of the minister as he sought to put across to me in English the full extent of his boss's discontent.

The ministerial conference ended very gloomily, reflecting the depth of disappointment. Many, possibly most, delegates thought that this time we had done it, that this time we were going to have a deal. People had come to do a deal and in the end it did not happen. Incidentally, the line-up of countries on either side of the argument over safeguards in 2008 gives the lie to one of the most commonly touted clichés surrounding the Doha negotiations on agriculture, which is that they are a struggle between rich and poor, developed and developing. The fight was really between those who want more open farm markets and those who – often for under-standable reasons – fear them.

Safeguards were a technical issue, but one that reflected underlying political concerns. Since the failure of 2008, the negotiations have been effectively on hold. With the global financial crisis, world leaders' attention, at least initially, switched elsewhere. Although the matter of safe-guards thwarted us in 2008, it is not the biggest issue separating members in 2013 as I prepare to stand down as Director-General. The biggest obstacle is a lack of consensus on the need to act multilaterally. Countries no longer see any urgency for a multilateral deal. Unfortunately, trade was not a political priority for the first Obama administration, and in his second presidential term, the focus seems to be on regional rather than multilateral deals. But it is not just the United States; the big guys in general think that they can go their own way and try to gain leverage through bilateral or regional initiatives. As I write, the European Union and the United States have just begun negotiations on what could be the biggest bilateral trade accord ever struck.

Breaking the deadlock

Some say that bilateral deals provide a faster route to trade opening as they allow participants to omit the most politically difficult issues such as agriculture and fisheries subsidies, anti-dumping rules or tariff peaks. Some argue it is easier to conclude deals when you can pick and choose your partners. For others, this proliferation is more driven by geopolitics than by economics.

On average, each member of the WTO belongs to no fewer than thirteen separate preferential trade agreements. This means that in addition to their multilateral commitments, WTO members on average have to manage an additional thirteen separate trade regimes. And the landscape is becoming further complicated by the launch of mega-regional deals such as the US-led Trans-Pacific Partnership (TPP), the EU–US Transatlantic Trade and Investment Partnership, the

ASEAN-led Regional Comprehensive Economic Partnership, and the China, Korea and Japan Free Trade Agreement. This cannot be the most efficient way to trade and to do business across national frontiers. Several problems arise. First, arrangements such as these impose trade costs. For the business community, for example, it is frustrating and costly to face multiple sets of rules of origin when supply chains stretch across several countries belonging to different trade pacts. What is more, the more pacts there are, the more diluted their benefits become for members. And while most preferential agreements do not appear to be built with the explicit intention of excluding or penalizing third parties, they can still generate geopolitical tensions.

Whatever the political or trade policy intent of regional and bilateral agreements, such pacts can create undesirable divergences in policy approaches that make it harder to build broader, more multilaterally based trading arrangements. Professor Jagdish Bhagwati of Columbia University has for many years warned that preferential agreements can have a negative impact on multilateral trade opening, and risk harming the weakest members of the trading system who are left out of these deals. This risk of policy divergence becomes more acute in today's world, where tariffs are increasingly an instrument of the past and non-tariff measures are the cutting edge of trade policy, as we saw in Chapter 2. The risk for the future is that we have a multilateral playing field overshadowed by the proliferation of divergent regulatory regimes.

Members of the WTO must face up to the reality of this growing contradiction between the desire for more trade opening and the reluctance to conclude a multilateral deal.

They can no longer bury their heads in the sand. They need to understand the root causes of their inability to advance multilateral trade opening and a regulatory agenda, and to build a collective response. Blaming others will not help. While it has become fashionable to say the WTO has too many members to agree on new rules, the reality is that the deadlock in the Doha Round is really due to disagreement among a small handful of advanced and emerging economies. As with the climate change negotiations, it is geopolitical in nature.

Agreement is still lacking on the balance of contributions and benefits between the United States, the European Union, Japan and the like on the one side, and India, China, Brazil and the like on the other side. Advanced economies argue that emerging economies have now 'emerged' and should therefore accept a trade regime that is similar to theirs. Emerging countries argue that they still face daunting development challenges that require flexibilities in the form of 'special and differential treatment'. This basically means that they should do less tariff cutting than the developed countries. Behind this conundrum lies a simple geopolitical question: are emerging countries 'rich countries with many poor people' or 'poor countries with many rich people'? Until and unless both sides agree on the answer, consensus in multilateral negotiations will remain elusive.

So WTO members need to address the different views as to what constitutes a fair balance of rights and obligations within the trading system, among members with different levels of development. What is the right share of concessions for advanced economies and emerging markets? What is the right degree of reciprocity among trade partners with similar levels of development and the right degree of flexibility that would allow weaker members to adjust to greater competition? It is clear that progress in multilateral trade negotiations, as in climate change negotiations, will require a political response to this political question.

Many ideas have been put forward for breaking the impasse in the trade negotiations. I will flag just a few that need urgent attention. The first is political leadership. Trade agreements need political leadership both at home and in Geneva. Governments strike trade agreements, not wise men, think tanks or directors-general. Government leaders must convince their electorates of the benefits of trade opening in a multilateral context. The time for technical work at the WTO is long past. It is the hour of politics. The problem lies with a handful of big countries, not with the bulk of the WTO membership. The smaller countries see clearly that multilateralism offers the only route for them to secure more trading opportunities under fairer conditions, but they lack the political leverage to bring the big players back to the negotiating table.

Furthermore, there needs to be a spirit of pragmatism and compromise among the big players. There has to be more give and take; there has to be more flexibility. And there has to be a spirit of realism. Asking for the moon and using empty rhetoric is normal in any negotiation, but the negotiations are past that. We must now seek realistic and creative solutions. To stand behind red negotiating lines waiting for others to move only breeds mistrust. In my view, there has to be agreement on three principles.

The first is that emerging countries must accept that, as they develop, they will align their level of international commitments to those of advanced economies. At the same time, advanced economies must recognize that emerging countries deserve long transition periods to converge towards common commitments. Finally, for the poorest countries, whether on trade or on climate change, the issue is less the level of commitments they may have to make in any agreement but more how to help them build the capacity to meet these commitments in the future and to be active members of the international family. If convergence could be found on these principles, I am convinced that the technicalities of trade, or environmental reforms such as those needed to tackle climate change, could rapidly emerge.

But more is needed. The approach in the WTO has been to seek to move step by step, gradually moving forward the parts of the Doha Round that are mature, and rethinking those where greater differences remain. This is important but it is no longer enough. WTO members also need to look at the real drivers of today's and tomorrow's world trade, at today's and tomorrow's obstacles to trade, at today's and tomorrow's trade patterns, at how to keep transforming trade into development, growth, jobs and poverty alleviation. In sum, they must equip the WTO with twenty-first-century software.

Since 2001, the world of international commerce has seen major transformations, whether in terms of WTO players, in terms of issues on the agenda or in geopolitical terms. The past decade or so has seen a strong rise in agricultural prices, so strong, in fact, that they have triggered two international food crises. Agriculture is the cornerstone of the Round. It is also the one area that is almost impossible to deal with in bilateral or regional negotiations. The impact of production subsidies cannot be neutralized for just one or even a handful of export markets; their effect is global. With the rise in food prices, the subsidizers, and particularly the US, given the nature of its subsidy system, have been under less pressure from their farm lobbies to provide production support. But this means that many leading developing countries, particularly Brazil, Argentina and South Africa, are unwilling to offer significant cuts in industrial tariffs in return for reductions in subsidies that the Americans or the Europeans are not even using. The surge in farm prices has changed the negotiating equation – the exchange rate, in the parlance of trade negotiators – at least for the time being.

Nevertheless, despite the current difficulties and complications, the goals set in Doha are still relevant. Curbing fishery subsidies that contribute to over-fishing, eliminating export subsidies, reducing industrial tariffs, cutting red tape at customs, expanding opportunities for vibrant services sectors or better integrating least-developed countries in the trading system can hardly be seen as irrelevant, either now or in the future. Reducing trade-distorting agricultural subsidies will become essential again as soon as world prices dip or stop rising strongly. What is more, these issues would not simply disappear if the WTO were to call a halt to the Doha Round – as some have suggested – and tried to launch new trade negotiations in some other format. It would end up facing the same dilemmas.

World in transition

The Doha Round embodies the transition between the old world and the new world that I witnessed in my eight years as

Director-General. I know why we launched the Round and I have seen the transformation in global trade that has been taking place since. Concluding the Doha Round is a political imperative. The objective – to rebalance the rules in favour of developing countries – must be reached. At stake is the very health of the multilateral trading system; failure would weigh heavily in other areas of multilateral negotiations, including on climate change.

As I write, members of the WTO are preparing for the December 2013 ministerial conference in Bali, Indonesia, where they will take fresh stock of the negotiations. I am hopeful that they will reach agreement in a number of areas, including trade facilitation and some elements of agriculture and special and differential treatment. If they do, these partial agreements could inject new life into the Round. But in the end, breaking the deadlock may require more. It may require combining the Doha Round with a new agenda that would be more attuned to topics that have become increasingly relevant since 2001. Many of these topics, including food security, energy and competition policy, have been discussed in earlier chapters.

In early 2012, I commissioned a twelve-strong panel of independent experts to take a look at the challenges facing the world trading system and to make recommendations. Their report – 'The Future of Trade: the Challenges of Convergence', published in April 2013 – confirmed the need to conclude the Doha Round for reasons that we have outlined. To facilitate this task, it called for re-examining the notions of reciprocity and flexibility as they are applied to the trade negotiations.

The idea that all countries should not 'face exactly the same set of obligations at a given point in time' was not questioned by the report. But while recognizing the legitimacy of differentiation, it urged a more 'dynamic approach'. Flexibility should be moulded to match the needs and capacities of individual members rather than being across-the-board exceptions and caveats for whole groups of countries. 'They should target specific challenges and not focus on categories of countries, and they should be time-specific. They also need to be monitored effectively to show that they are helping with convergence', the report recommended.

The report also noted concerns about the prevalence of corruption in many parts of the world, and the destructive effect this has not just on economies, but also on the fabric of society itself. The WTO could play its part in mitigating this cancer. Greater respect for transparency in trade policy and administration would be one contribution. At the end of the day, transparency is precisely a core principle of the WTO.

It also noted that current arrangements for international co-operation in competition policy are fragmented between different domestic and international organizations and leave gaps in the fabric of global economic governance, including that of trade. By resuming work in this area, the WTO could help plug some of these gaps. Similarly, in investment policy, the report saw a growing need for the WTO to get involved in setting international rules and regulations.

Trade and foreign direct investment (FDI) are becoming linked in new ways as more and more trade is made up of components in value chains that span national boundaries. 'Trade and FDI have become two sides of the same coin', the report said. But there is no international organization that deals with both these aspects of globalization. In fact, investment tends to be handled on a bilateral basis. As in the case of competition policy, this lack of multilateral rules creates a gap in governance and undermines efforts towards global policy coherence and convergence. And if there is one theme that stands out in the report, it is the need for policy convergence, a theme that has been at the heart of this book. We need convergence in four main areas: convergence of the trade regimes of WTO members; convergence of the non-multilateral regimes with the multilateral trading system; convergence between trade and other public policies; and convergence of trade and other domestic policies.

Convergence in the trade regimes of WTO members in line with their evolving economic and social development embraces the notion – mentioned above – that flexibilities built into trade agreements to help poorer developing countries – special and differential treatment – must have convergence as their goal. The aim must be to assist countries in bringing their trading environments and regulations into line with those in other member countries.

Convergence between non-multilateral regimes, such as bilateral and plurilateral trade agreements, and the multilateral trading system is equally important. Unless there is convergence between these different trade accords, the world will face a 'spaghetti bowl' of regulations that in the end will prove a barrier to growth through trade.

When it comes to convergence between trade and other public policies related to trade, I am thinking specifically of non-tariff measures, such as technical standards. As we saw in Chapter 2, these can present an increasing obstacle to open trade.

Finally, there has to be convergence of trade with other domestic policies, such as education, innovation and social safety nets. Without this convergence, countries will not develop the human capacity needed to compete effectively in international markets. Without this convergence, they will not create the political environment in which there will be public support for open markets, particularly at times of economic crises.

What has been achieved so far in the Doha Round negotiations, and what a successful conclusion would add, amount to a major array of potential benefits at a global level. It would mean more trade and better trade rules, providing opportunities for investment and jobs. It would mean greater opportunities for the poorest. It would mean for the first time placing development at the heart of the global trading system.

But, above all, it would mean that the spirit of global trade co-operation is still alive. It would mean that governments and parliaments alike believe trade is better regulated at the global level than through a myriad of bilateral agreements that have limited value for today's global supply chains; that they still believe it is worth investing in multilateralism; that they want to foster the predictability and stability of world trade at a turbulent time. This is why political leaders must make it a priority to conclude the Round and reap these benefits.

Epilogue

In July 2013, I bade farewell to the WTO's General Council, the major decision-making body of the organization. It was an opportunity for me to look back at my eight years as Director-General and to look forward to the challenges that lie ahead for the multilateral trading system.

As I have already strongly asserted in this book, negotiating trade opening is not the only function of the WTO, but it is clearly one of its central functions.

Because the latest round of trade negotiations – the Doha Round – has not yet been concluded, some might be tempted to say that the organization is in crisis, that trade multilateralism does not function, that the WTO has become irrelevant. I believe the reality is much more complex.

To begin with, I do not think the debate is about the relevance of the WTO. It is about its credibility. This credibility stems from the capacity to deliver results. And achieving multilateral trade opening today is not an easy task.

Opening trade and crafting multilateral rules has been severely affected by the profound shifts in geopolitics and economics. The former two-speed model of a world divided between developed and developing countries no longer reflects today's economic realities. We must find a new balance in a multidimensional membership if we are to achieve multilateral trade opening. This challenge is compounded by short-term politics that are becoming

186

increasingly incompatible with the medium and longer-term goal setting needed for designing consistent trade policies.

Trade opening has been further dented by the biggest economic crisis since the 1930s, which has left millions unemployed in advanced economies and which is now hindering the sustainability of growth in emerging economies. I also believe it is too easy to say that trade multilateralism does not function. We saw trade multilateralism work at the Hong Kong Ministerial Conference in 2005. And as I write this, I am confident that we will see it work again at the Bali Ministerial Conference at the end of 2013, with the successful conclusion of a deal on trade facilitation, together with some development and agriculture issues, and even the possibility of extending the coverage of the Information Technology Agreement.

We have also seen multilateralism work in the accession negotiations, which brought eleven new members into the WTO family during my tenure as Director-General: large economies, such as Russia, Saudi Arabia, Vietnam and Ukraine; small economies, such as Tajikistan and Montenegro; and five least-developed countries: Samoa, Vanuatu, Tonga, Laos and Cape Verde. Together, they are equivalent to an economy the size of Germany.

In spite of these achievements, I often hear that the way forward is to abandon the WTO and simply move to plurilateral or regional arrangements. But we know that behind the headlines of the launching of mega-regional deals, as some refer to them, lie tremendous difficulties and sometimes even no final deal at all.

We need to recognize that the issue is not trade opening in the WTO as opposed to trade opening outside the WTO. The issue today is with the difficulties involved in trade opening. Domestic trade politics have become more difficult and trade deals have become more complex because the nature of obstacles to trade has evolved. We are no longer just negotiating the reduction of tariffs but also of non-tariff barriers, which have gained enormous importance. We also need to recognize that trade is just one instrument for generating growth and creating jobs. It is not the only instrument. And it is an instrument for, not a weapon against, the well-being of all.

The fact that non-tariff barriers are becoming the main obstacle to trade requires us to rethink the way we deal with them. How do we ensure that we limit the negative effects on trade of measures legitimately taken to protect consumers? The WTO is not a regulatory agency for the vast majority of non-tariff measures, but it is well placed to become a platform where the convergence of these measures could be monitored in the future.

Finally, I do believe the way we conduct multilateral negotiations could be improved and that we could learn from the practices of other international organizations. Much time could be saved in the negotiating process if, after an initial phase of defining objectives and principles, the WTO Secretariat was tasked to mobilize its expertise to table proposals around which the negotiations would take place. WTO members would of course take the final decision.

These eight years have seen the building of a stronger institution. The WTO is now an institution, which is more than an organization. Beyond the benefits that it provides to its members, the WTO, as an institution, is an asset in itself, a global public good that each and every one of its members must nurture. Of course the director-general represents the system and should always care about the system. But it cannot be that the 'DG lives on Venus', the planet of a global public good, and 'members live on Mars', the planet where members fight for their individual interests. Each and every member of the WTO must look beyond its interests and also care about this institution, both as owners and as the stakeholders that they are.

In these eight years I have also seen the political economy of trade opening better integrated into a set of domestic and international policies. This is an important step forward in the challenge of 'convergence'. Support for more open trade will not be sustained without ensuring greater fairness between the winners and losers of trade opening, and without more convergence on the values-based preferences that lie behind differences in non-tariff measures. Achieving this new vision of the 'Geneva Consensus' remains a challenge.

clean technology and services,
and climate change, 115
competition and energy resource
dual pricing for domestic and
conditions of trade in, 112
export restrictions, 114, 119
geographical concentration of
and international co-operation,
renewable resources, 112, 115,
scarce and non-renewable nature
share of trade, 111
sovereignty and strategic
subsidies for renewable, 116
supply-side players in, 115
Enhanced Integrated Framework, 45
and public policies, 56
environmental goods and services,
58, 61, 65, 119

environmental protection, 55–67
    international accords on, 56
    regulations for, 58
    and trade regulation, 61
ethical standards, 154;
    see also labour standards,
    standards
Europe
    and governance, 7–9
    institutions and tools of
        governance, 7
    integration of, 7
European Coal and Steel
    Community, 148
European Union, 117, 148, 153
    Common Agricultural Policy, 74
    and the Doha Round, 176, 178
    Everything but Arms initiative,
        42
    exchange rate volatility in, 125
    and Rwanda, 49
exchange rates, 122–30
    adjustments, 123
    Bretton Woods system, 127–8
    and financial crises, 123
    and international companies, 126
    misalignments of, 126, 129
    and policy coherence, 127–30
    and price elasticity, 125
    stability of, 128–9
    and trade, 124–30
    and uncertainty, 122
    volatility of, 124, 127, 129
Expert Group on Trade Finance, 51,
    53
export subsidies, 74, 77
exports, 20

194